JOB DESCRIPTIONS FOR TODAY'S MINISTRY

In the African Methodist Episcopal Zion Church

The steps of a good man are ordered by the Lord, and He delights in his way.
Psalm 37:23

JOB DESCRIPTIONS FOR TODAY'S MINISTRY

In the African Methodist Episcopal Zion Church

The steps of a good man are ordered by the Lord, and He delights in his way.
Psalm 37:23

Triple J Publishing
Sanford, North Carolina

Ophelia W. Livingston

Job Descriptions for Today's Ministry
In the African Methodist Episcopal Zion Church

Requests for information should be addressed to:
OWL Risk Management Consulting, LLC

"Scripture quotations are from The Holy Bible, English Standard Version®, copyright © 2001 by Crossway Bibles, a publishing ministry of Good News Publishers. Used by permission. All rights reserved."

Scripture quotations designated (NIV) are from THE HOLY BIBLE: NEW INTERNATIONAL VERSION. Copyright © 1973, 1978, 1984 by International Bible Society. All rights are reserved by Zondervan Publishing House. The "NIV" and "New International Version" trademarks are registered in the United States Patent and Trademark Office by:

International Bible Society
1820 Jet Stream Drive
Colorado Springs, Colorado 80921, USA
In the US, phone: (719) 488-9200

Cover Design by Triple J Publishing
Thirteen-Digit ISBN: 978-0-9840853-0-9
Religion/Spirituality/Administration
Edited by Barbara S. Keller

Triple J Publishing, Sanford, North Carolina
© 2010 by Triple J Publishing
Printed in the United States of America

All rights are reserved under International Copyright Law. No part of this publication may be reproduced, stored in a retrieval system, or transmitted in any form or by any means – electronic, mechanical, photocopy, recording, or any other – except for brief quotation in printed reviews, without the prior permission of the publisher.

For more information go:
Website: http://www.owlrisk.com
Blog: www.owlrisk.blogspot.com
E-mail at owlivingston@owlrisk.com
Toll-free: 1-866-579-7475

About the Author

Ophelia W. Livingston, is President and Executive Director of OWL Risk Management Consulting, LLC a consulting company dedicated to meeting the needs of small businesses, non-profits and churches in the areas of 501(c)3, checklist management and nonprofit audit compliance. We have dedicated ourselves to helping those who are called into leadership with the Body of Christ. She also works with small businesses in the area of IT audit compliance.

In addition:

Ophelia's credentials are as follows: Bachelor of Science, Business Administration, University of North Carolina at Greensboro; Master of Business Administration (MBA) – Information Security, Salem International University; Master of Science in Information Systems (MSIS), University of Fairfax. Livingston is a Level Four Church Consultant completing training for Society of Church Consulting. All of the resources are a result of extensive research into laws that govern non-profits (tax-exempt) and churches. OWL Risk Management Consulting, LLC has compiled effective and user-friendly manuals, how-to-books and compliance guides, all designed to protect and empower your church, ministry or non-profit organizations.

Other Books by Triple J Publishing

Church Risk Management Guide for Today's Ministry

A Music Ministry Handbook for Music Leaders

All The Praise: 52 Weeks of Praise Devotions found at www.createspace.com/3401076

Praise Journal: Taking Your Praise Notes found at www.createspace.com/3422310

Contact us at 1-866-579-7475 or www.praisediet.com

Table of Contents

For more information go: Website: http://www.owlrisk.com Blog: www.owlrisk.blogspot.com E-mail at owlivingston@owlrisk.com Toll-free: 1-866-579-7475 About the Author iv

About the Author v

Other Books by Triple J Publishing vi

Table of Contents viii

Preface xiii

Introduction 1

Understanding the Purpose of Church Job Descriptions 3

    What Is A Job Description? 4

    The best job descriptions are living and breathing documents that are updated as responsibilities change. 4

    What Is the Title? 5

    What Is the Ministry or Department 5

    What Is Job or Position Summary 5

    What Is Job Content 5

    What Are Knowledge, Skills and Abilities? 5

    What Are Qualifications? 6

    What Is the Acknowledgement of Review? 6

    Job Descriptions and Church Ministry Development 6

    Why Is There A Need for Job Descriptions? 6

Verbs Used In Job Descriptions 8

History of the Black Church 11

    Historical Black Denominations 12

History of the African Methodist Episcopal Zion Church 13

    The Local Churches 14

The Meaning of the A.M.E. Zion Church Logo 15

The Meaning of African Methodist Episcopal Zion	16
Definitions	17
The First Church Organization	21
Definition of "Organization"	22
Benefits of Good Organization	23
The First Biblical Organization: Exodus 18:13-27	26
Called Versus Staff	27
Staff	27
Organizational Chart	30
Christian Education Department (CED) Organizational Chart	31
Women's Home and Overseas Missionary Society Organizational Chart	32
What Are Church Boards?	33
Boards	35
Trustee	37
Steward	39
Preacher's Steward	41
Poor Steward	43
General Claims Steward	45
Junior Steward	47
Class Leader	49
Deaconess	51
Stewardess	53
Lay Activities (Council)	55
Local Director of Evangelism	57
Christian Education Board Member	59
Directors of Christian Education	63
Superintendent of the Sunday Church School	65
Sunday Church School Teacher	67

Missionary Society 69

Women's Home and Overseas Missionary Society 71

Local Coordinator of the Young Adult Missionary Department 73

Local Coordinator of the Young Adult Missionary Officers 75

Local Church Staff Member 77

Administrative Assistant - Local Church Staff Member 79

Music Director or Minister of Music - Local Church Staff 81

Church Musician - Local Church Staff Member 83

Church Secretary - Local Church Staff Member 85

Church Sexton - Local Church Staff Member 87

Church Treasurer - Local Church Staff Member 89

Worship 91

Greeter - Local Church Member ....

Ushe Local Church Member ....

Church Committee 99

Committees 101

What are Committees? 101

What are Rotating Committees? 102

Do's and Don'ts Tips of Committee Meetings 104

Acolyte Chairperson - Local Church Member 93

Acolyte – Local Church Member 94

Budget/Finance Committee 105

Bulletin Board Committee 106

Culinary Arts Committee 107

Estimating Salary Committee 108

Evangelism Committee 109

Floral Guild 110

Worship Committee 111

x

A Basic Guide To Do's and Don'ts of Church Interview Questions 113
Do's and Don'ts Etiquettes of Church Interview Questions 117
Notes 119
Notes 120
Notes 121
Notes 122
Notes 123
Notes 124
Notes 125
Join OWL Risk Management Consulting's Monthly Newsletter 126

Preface

Job Descriptions for Today's Ministry - In the African Methodist Episcopal Zion Church was written to provide a comprehensive reference for church leaders nationally.

According to Psalm 37:23, "The steps of a good man are ordered by the Lord, and He delights in his way". Do you have conflict in your ministry because there is no clear understanding as to who should be performing a particular function? Did someone in your ministry or organization quit because of hurt feelings because a role or function lacked clarity? This book will address how to effectively write a clear and concise job role for your church ministry.

Before developing church descriptions and job functions, there is a need to formally establish a church organizational chart. To achieve oversight and accountability, a church organizational chart equips clergy with the requirements for church governance. By developing a church organizational chart, clergies are standardizing effective communication. Organizational charts provide clergies with information that can be used as a baseline for effective and efficient planning, budgeting and collaborating. Good charts allow clergy to organize their ministerial staff with clear responsibilities, titles and lines of authority. An example of an official organizational structure is found in the Book of Exodus, Chapter 18. Jethro, the father-in-law of Moses, was wise enough to see that Moses needed help to prevent burnout and ruining the plans God had given him. Therefore, Jethro laid out a structural plan and is noted for being history's first recorded management consultant. He helped Moses see that organization and structure are essential to effective operation. Understanding one's role in any organization brings forth a sense of accomplishment when completing tasks.

The source of much of this text is the local church and the expectations of the functions within the local church. The writer is a "child of the church," having grown up in a Christian and church-centered family, and having been an active church member since professing faith in Christ at the age of ten. However, the main ideas in this book come from sources other than church. They have been found through study, experience and observation of the local AME Zion church.

One of the most important documents a church can have is an organizational chart, providing a high-level overview of the pecking order of your ministry. As always, my immediate family members have me in their debt beyond my ability to repay.

Ophelia W. Livingston

OWL Risk Management Consulting, LLC.

Sanford, NC

Introduction

The primary purpose of a job description is to identify the **essential functions** of a specified position. A job description describes the purpose, duties, responsibilities, tasks, and relationships of a particular job. Without a written formal job description, it is difficult to hold a staff member or volunteer accountable for performing the duties of his/her position. Without a written formal job description, it is impossible to measure or evaluate the performance of the person performing the job role or function.

A job description should be written in terms of the position itself and should not be based on the capabilities of any individual. All job descriptions are summaries containing enough information to be useful and should not be confusing or misleading to the applicants.

#	Function	Description
1	Title	The title of job position/role should be clear and consistent with similar positions in the ministry.
2	**Ministry/Department**	Department or ministry to which job role belongs
3	**Job Position Summary**	Two or three sentences in length
4	**Line of authority**	Title of person applicant will report to. Use job titles (i.e., pastor, church business administrator), not specific names (i.e., Pastor James, Sally Jo).
5	**Principal Duties and Responsibilities**	The first three functions should be the core duties and responsibilities
6	**Other Duties and Responsibilities**	This section contains responsibilities and important duties performed occasionally or in addition to the essential functions of the position.
7	**Knowledge, Skills and Abilities Required**	Entries that support the principle duties and responsibilities. • Knowledge – Listing the level of education, training and experience an individual should have at minimum to be considered qualified for the position. • Skills – Specific skills, such as the ability to perform public speaking, read music, ability to use software applications such as manipulate spreadsheets. Avoid specifying or naming products unless a specific program or application is needed. • Abilities – Describe the manual requirements such as ability to lift 50 pounds. If position is for Security, use descriptive language as "the ability to walk and run will be essential."
8	**Qualifications**	A short summary can be substituted here instead of the lengthy description above.
9	**Acknowledgement of Review**	The applicant signs and dates this form indicting he/she has read and understands the description of the general content of and the requirements for performing this job.

Table 1: Job Description Matrix

As your ministry or non-profit moves toward governance and best practices, you should consider standardizing and using a job description format. A standard format is useful as your ministry or non-profit grows allowing leaders and board members to quickly and easily incorporate new positions throughout the organization. By using a job description template, it is easily adaptable and modifiable in any area. On page 1, up to nine sections may be in a job description template and are listed in *table 1*.

Understanding the Purpose of Church Job Descriptions

There are mounds of work to do in the ministry of the church. Unless jobs are described and defined, people will not be able to work effectively. Conflict between groups and individuals can result, or workers may not be very happy in what they do. People know what to do or should do as the Holy Spirit guides them. Ministries can become so busy that leaders cannot think through the organizational structure to know how to use their time and talents most effectively.

Just like everyday workplace, a church has a number of jobs to be completed. For effective and efficient church leadership management it is better to develop position descriptions that:

- **Clarify expectations**: A well-defined position can communicate what is needed in any job in the church, how a person in a ministry will be evaluated (whether formally or informally), and how leaders will know the work is getting done.

- **Set boundaries**: There is a difference between expecting a person to do a few things well (very efficiently) and doing a little of everything (very inefficiently). Job descriptions can set important boundaries between workers so that they are not taking over other people's work.

- **Define lines of authority**: People want to know to whom they are accountable and why. People want to know what their responsibilities are. Workers also will be less likely to send mixed signals about whose direction to follow, and at what point the supervisor takes charge.

- **Eliminate work and ministry conflicts**: With clearly set boundaries and defined lines of authority, the likelihood that people will move into conflict is significantly reduced. Workers will respect and honor each other and understand how each person is part of a team to advance the Lord's work.

It is essential to write a description for each work function in a standardized format so that church staff, volunteers, church leaders and the congregation will understand the main elements of every job in churches and ministries. These descriptions should be put into a church policy and procedures manual so that, if disputes or misunderstandings arise, everyone has the same information to guide them.

What Is A Job Description?

The process of developing a job description helps a ministry or non-profit articulate the most important outcomes needed to perform a particular job. A job description is also a communication tool that defines boundaries of that person's responsibilities.

A well-written job description tells a staff member or a volunteer member where his job fits within the overall ministry or non-profit organization. Job descriptions are written statements that describe the:

- duties,
- responsibilities,
- most important contributions and outcomes needed from a position,
- required qualifications of candidates, and
- reporting relationship of a particular job (who the person reports to).

Job descriptions clearly identify and spell out the responsibilities of a specific job. Job descriptions also include information about working conditions, tools, equipment used, knowledge and skills needed, and relationships with other positions.

The best job descriptions are living and breathing documents that are updated as responsibilities change.

Effectively developed, job descriptions are communication tools that are significant to a church's, ministry's or nonprofit's success. Poorly written job descriptions, on the other hand, add to church confusion, hurt communication, and make church staff or volunteers feel as if they do not know what is expected from them. A living and breathing document is one that is reviewed and updated periodically because duties and responsibilities may change throughout the years.

What Is the Title?

A title is a label used to describe a specific set of activities, responsibilities, duties or tasks within a ministry.

What Is the Ministry or Department

The functions or groups are made up of several ministries in the church and they all work for the evangelization of the people of God. The word "ministry" literally means "service". In the Christian life, it refers to specific roles, tasks and works of service designated by the church.

What Is Job or Position Summary

The Job or Position Summary briefly describes the duties and responsibilities of the position. This summary should explain the basic reporting structure and the "what and why" to be accomplished in the position. It should be written in two or three sentences.

What Is Job Content

The Job Content section contains two sub-categories: "Principal Duties" and "Other Duties and Responsibilities." The **Principal Duties and Responsibilities** contains the *essential functions* mentioned in the Introduction. *Essential Functions* must contain the core functions of the position. There should be no more than 12 core or essential functions of the position. An *essential function* must meet at least one of the following criteria:

1. The reason the position exists is to perform this duty. Removing this function would fundamentally change this position.
2. A limited number of people are available to perform this function.
3. Expertise is required to perform this job function.

The **Other Duties and Responsibilities** section covers other duties that are not considered an essential function of the position.

What Are Knowledge, Skills and Abilities?

This section may break out into two or three subsections. Every entry in this section must be supported by the Principal Duties and Responsibilities section.

- **Knowledge:** The level of education, experience and training an individual must have at minimum to be considered qualified for the position.

- **Skills:** Specific skills such as the ability to administer, execute and strategize certain tasks. Avoid using program names such as i.e., (Microsoft Word, Logos Church Management software, etc.) unless knowledge of that specific program is essential.
- **Abilities:** List each individual requirement. Remember, every entry in this section must be directly supported in the **Principal Duties and Responsibilities** section.

What Are Qualifications?

Qualifications prove that an individual has gained the knowledge and developed certain skills. Qualifications are derived from what is required to perform the duties and responsibilities. This is where you can list any required degrees, certifications, years of experience, and licenses needed to perform the job.

What Is the Acknowledgement of Review?

This section is optional on the job description template. It is a disclaimer used against any litigation that may occur in your ministry. Furthermore, it provides documented proof that the position appointed to or interviewed for is understood by the clergy, church leader, staff, consultant or volunteer member.

Unlike work in the secular corporation, a church's official position description does not require a salary disclosure unless denomination has a compensation chart, especially for ordained ministers. A response to an initial question or a section of the job interview may spell out specific compensation issues.

Job Descriptions and Church Ministry Development

Job descriptions have the ability to provide clear expectations and boundaries for a church's total ministry. Job descriptions assist church leaders, church staff and volunteer members understand the nature of role positions based on the following:

Why Is There A Need for Job Descriptions?

A job description has a defined place in the church's or ministry's mission and strategy. As positions are filled, clergies, church leaders and lay ministers understand how they advance the mission or agenda of the gospel and the church, *not* their own. Church members also understand why certain positions are essential for church strategy and growth even if the work is not important to them.

As a church or ministry expands, diminishes or even changes its DNA culture, jobs can be redefined or retooled as needed. This method is called *Church Process Re-structuring or CPR)*. CPR is a church leadership approach to improve efficiency and effectiveness of roles that exist within the church. A ministry's strategy can identify certain positions to be created, changed or eliminated.

New ministries can be identified and new work roles can be developed. In this way, existing employees can be given the opportunity to advance, specialize or focus. Or, as situations change for church staff, they can cut back on their hours or their responsibilities.\

A job description should be filed electronically and on paper as part of the personnel evaluation process. A person's job performance can be compared to stated responsibilities. Job descriptions ultimately are beneficial because they will help people in the ministry to do an effective job and help the church fulfill God's call to the ministry.

Verbs Used In Job Descriptions

Action verbs are useful in concisely stating the functions of jobs. Concise writing is easier for church members to understand. An example of an action verb and its definition is ***Maintain: keep in an existing state.***

accommodate	clean	direct
achieve	clear	discuss
acquire	climb	disseminate
act	collaborate	distinguish
adapt	collect	distribute
address	combine	document
adjust	communicate	draft
administer	compile	drive
adopt	complete	edit
advise	compose	eliminate
allocate	conduct	encourage
analyze	confer	enforce
apply	consolidate	ensure
appoint	construct	establish
appraise	consult	evaluate
approve	control	execute
arrange	convert	exhibit
as	cook	expand
assemble	coordinate	expedite
assess	correlate	explore
assign	correspond	extract
assist	counsel	facilitate
assume	create	file
attain	customize	forecast
attract	delegate	formulate
audit	deliver	furnish
augment	demonstrate	gather
authorize	design	generate
budget	determine	govern
calculate	develop	guide
circulate	devise	handle
clarify	devote	highlight

hire	plan	search
identify	predict	secure
illustrate	prepare	select
implement	present	serve
improve	preside	service
improvise	prevent	sign
incorporate	process	simplify
increase	produce	sell
influence	program	solicit
inform	promote	solve
initiate	propose	specify
inspect	provide	stimulate
instruct	publicize	strategize
interact	publish	streamline
interface	push	strengthen
interpret	pull	study
interview	quantify	submit
introduce	recognize	suggest
investigate	recommend	summarize
issue	reconcile	supervise
lead	record	support
lift	recruit	systematize
maintain	redesign	teach
manage	reduce	test
market	refer	trace
modify	refine	train
monitor	regulate	transcribe
motivate	reinforce	transfer
negotiate	repair	translate
notify	reorganize	transmit
obtain	report	troubleshoot
operate	represent	type
originate	research	update
organize	resolve	upgrade
oversee	restructure	validate
participate	review	verify
perform	schedule	walk
persuade	screen	weld

Christ harmoniously incorporates, orders, and sustains all nature. His omnipotent and omniscient powers guarantee that the universe is under His control and is not chaotic.

History of the Black Church

A good way to understand a people is to study their religion, for religion is addressed to the most sacred schedule of values around us. The historical development that marks the various African American denominations provides the physical structures through which the Black church lives out its doctrines and beliefs.

The black church continues to be a source of support for members of the African American community. In the case of the Black Church, the genesis of the first splintered movement began in 1786 at St. George's Episcopal Methodist Church in Philadelphia. When Absalom Jones and Richard Allen kneeled down to pray to a God they knew not to be a "respecter of persons," they were rudely interrupted and told they had to go up into the balcony, separated from their white congregants. The event spurred Jones to eventually leave in 1793 to form the African Methodist Episcopal Church (AME) denomination. Similar incidents of isolation and discontent caused James Varick, Peter Williams and Charles Rush to charter the African Methodist Episcopal Zion Church (AME Zion) in 1796 in New York. The South was no different. The then Colored Methodist Episcopalians, now known as the Christian Methodist Episcopalians (CME) was formed as a result of a schism over the theology slavery between northern and southern states. Black congregants formed their own denomination in order to minister to their needs, culture and experiences.

The blending of theological reflections with modern issues and denominations structures is clearly articulated by Baptists. In the 1800's, 150 Black Baptist pastors met in Montgomery, Alabama to form the Baptist Mission Convention. By 1895 it had merged with two other conventions to form the National Baptist Convention of the United States of America. Until then, previous attempts to form all Black Baptist church associations and conventions were not allowed.

Throughout the ages, the African American people have institutionalized the gathering of people to worship and created several historical black denominations.

Historical Black Denominations

African Union First Colored Methodist Protestant Church and Connection   chartered in 1813
    Spencer Churches 1st independent black denomination

African Methodist Episcopal Church   formed in 1816

African Methodist Episcopal Zion Church   founded in 1796, officially formed in 1821

Christian Methodist Episcopal Church   formed in 1870

National Baptist Convention, USA, Inc   formed in 1895

Apostolic Faith Mission   formed in 1906

Church of God in Christ   formed in 1907

Pentecostal Assemblies of God   founded in 1908, officially formed in 1912

National Baptist Convention of America, Inc   formed in 1915

United House of Prayer for All People   formed in 1919, incorporated in 1925

African Orthodox Church   formed in 1919

Spiritual Israel Church and Its Army   formed in 1925

Progressive National Baptist Convention   formed in 1961

National Missionary Baptist Convention of America   formed in 1988

http://en.wikipedia.org/wiki/Black_church#Historically_black_denominations

History of the African Methodist Episcopal Zion Church

The African Methodist Episcopal Zion Church is one of the many Methodist denominations that traces its roots to the Methodist revival movement within the Church of England begun by John Wesley and others. This movement would eventually become a separate denomination, the Methodist Church. Methodist was organized as a denomination within the United States as the Methodist Episcopal Church.

Out of this American manifestation of Methodism, the A.M.E. Zion Church would be born.

Under the leadership of such men as James Varick, George Collins, Charles Anderson and Christopher Rush, they drew up the doctrines and discipline of the African Methodist Episcopal Church in America. The men elected a number of elders, organized a national body in 1821 and James Varick was consecrated as the first bishop in 1822. There are three distinctive heritage points of Zion Methodist.

1. Zion Methodism grew out of the merciless enslavement of our African forebears. They were kidnapped from their native land, chained and shackled, shipped as beasts in deplorable conditions to a strange and distant land, having no family, no culture and no language. Yet, our fathers and mothers were confronted by the Lord God, through Jesus Christ, in the cotton fields and every place of the humiliation and degradation revealing to them that He would always be with them as He had been with them in the past. When Jesus, upon whom the Spirit of the Lord had descended, was preached at John Street Methodist Church, they united with that fellowship. However, bigotry and oppressively cruel barriers confronted them. The Spirit of the Lord led them in the establishment of Zion Chapel where the gospel of His Redeeming grace could be purely preached and His vindicating and liberating influences could be experienced. Taking with them the doctrines, discipline and polity of the Methodist Church, they proceeded in the establishment of Zion Methodism. They believed that God had called them out of their

bondage and had chosen them to be His people and the channel of His redeeming love for all people.

2. We believe and understand today that, in the Divine Economy, Zion Methodism is to make disciples of all persons throughout the earth, to bring good news to the poor, to proclaim release to the captive, recovery of sight to the blind, to let the oppressed go free and to proclaim the Year of the Lord's favor.

3. We are to continue this mission until Christ, God's Son, shall come again.

A.M.E. Zion Churches are located on these continents:
Africa, South America, North America, Asia, Europe

Africa	Namibia, Angola, Malawi, Mozambique, Nigeria, South Africa, Ivory Coast, Togo, Liberia, Ghana
North America	Bahamas, Virgin Islands, Jamaica, Trinidad-Tobago, Barbados, Canada, United States
South America	Brazil, Colombia, Guyana, Venezuela
Asia	India
Europe	Great Britain

Table 2: Five Continent Locations for A.M.E. Zion Churches

In the A.M.E. Zion Church there are four major categories and seven committees listed for all positions held in a local church. The four major categories include:

- Boards
- Missionaries
- Church Staff
- Worship Leaders

The seven committees include:
- Budget/Finance
- Bulletin Board
- Calendar
- Culinary Arts
- Estimating Salary
- Evangelism
- Floral Guild
- Worship

The Local Churches

The Local Churches are the cornerstones of The A.M.E. Zion Connection. The Pastor is ordained and appointed by the Bishop to a Local Church. Pastors are to preach and teach the Gospel of Jesus Christ by knowing both Old and New Testaments and continue in Kingdom Building. Pastors are to also pursue education and be trained in administration.

<u>Job Descriptions</u>

The Meaning of the A.M.E. Zion Church Logo

The triangle represents the Father, the Son and the Holy Spirit, which is called Holy Trinity.
- The **"V"** represents the victory and leadership of James Varick.
- The Latin cross represents Christianity.
- The **"A"** refers to the African background.
- The **"M"** represents Methodist for Christ who they love.
- The **"E"** means that whoever goes to the church will be overseen by Bishops.
- The **"Z"** represents Zion.

The Meaning of African Methodist Episcopal Zion

African: Means that the church will be led by the sons and daughters of Africa, and equality is a goal.

Methodist: Methodism emphasizes the need for order and consistency in personal and public faith.

Episcopal: The Bishops are chosen by the common church and oversee the denomination. The Bishops have an international connection. Today the A.M.E Zion church is operated on five continents.

Zion: Is used in the Bible to describe the church of God. Zion was put into the name in 1848.

Job Descriptions

Definitions

Affiliate Membership – persons who are members of other African Methodist Episcopal (A.M.E.) Zion churches outside the area who desire a local church home. The affiliate is counted as a member of the home church.

ArmorBearer – is a servant, anointed by God to serve as a leader of the kingdom of God. He/She is called to walk with his/her leader, assisting in any way necessary, to cause his/her leaders "God Given Vision" to come to pass; he/she is faithful, humble, loyal and trustworthy.

Chain of Command – the plan of organization suggested to Moses by his father-in-law, Jethro in Exodus 18:13-27.

Committees – a group of people officially delegated by the Pastor-in-Charge to perform a function, such as mentoring, reporting, negotiating or acting on a matter.

CPR – Church Process Re-structuring, see page 7

Essential Function – job duties that are required to complete the job tasks.

Ex-Officio - describes someone who has a right because of an office held, such as being allowed to sit on a committee simply because one is president of the corporation.

Exhorter – a layperson who has delivered a trial discourse, shall be a member of and subject to the Quarterly Conference. He/She shall report to the Quarterly and District Conference. He/She can obtain a license to exhort.

Good standing – attends faithfully the means of grace

Job Descriptions

Job Description – a written description of the duties for which a person is responsible.

Job Performance Standards – the degree to which a church worker is working according to the job description.

Lay Council – an organized body of lay people (non-clergy person) in the Zion Methodism whose responsibility it is to disseminate information to create a greater awareness and understanding of the polity and practice of the African Methodist Episcopal (A.M.E.) Zion Church.

Local Preacher – recommended by a majority of the District Conference upon the recommendation of the Quarterly Conference of which he/she is a member.

1. Candidates for local preacher's licenses must successfully complete and pass a written examination on the first year course of study required for local preachers.
2. For renewal – candidate must successfully complete and pass a written examination on the second year course of study required for local preachers.

Means of Grace – by "means of grace" outward signs, words, or actions, ordained of God, and appointed for this end, to be the ordinary channels whereby he might convey to men, preventing, justifying, or sanctifying grace, that a sacrament is "an outward sign of inward grace, and a means whereby we receive the same." Also, as the ministry of the Word and the public and private worship of the God: and further, ye shall provide that he/she shall read the Holy Scriptures, and learn the Lord's Prayer, the Ten Commandments, the Apostles' Creed, the Catechism, and all things which a Christian ought to know and believe to his/her soul's health, in order that he/she may be brought up to lead a virtuous and holy life, remembering always that Baptism doth represent upon us that inward purity which disposeth us to follow the example of our Savior Christ; that as he died and rose again for us, so should we, who are baptized, die unto sin and rise again unto righteousness.

Job Descriptions

Member in Good Standing or Member in Full Connection – a member, minister or layperson who has been converted and accepted the Christ way of life. He/She has the privilege of voting, and attending the Quarterly Conference and is entitled all spiritual privileges.

Preacher on Trial in Full Connection – One who has been employed in the regular itinerant works on circuits or stations, or as an instructor in institutionalized learning, for two successive years from the time he/she was received on trial. He/She may be admitted into full connection in the Annual Conference after given satisfactory evidence of knowledge of conference course of study and after examination.

Probation or **probatory** – a period of time (six months or longer) before a person is allowed full membership. A probationer cannot vote and cannot be a member of the Quarterly Conference. He/She is entitled all spiritual privileges.

Solid Piety – has moral character and spiritual maturity

Term Limits – members appointed to the Deaconess Board are appointed for life. All other job roles in the church have a one-year term limit and shall be confirmed at the Quarterly Conference.

Transfer – persons who transfer with full membership from another church

Trustees, Local Church Board of – A group of persons, nominated by the pastor and elected by the Quarterly Conference, who is responsible for the supervision and all of the property and equipment owned by the local church.

WH&OM Society – Women's Home and Overseas Missionary. The women's arm of Zion Methodism responsible for promoting missionary activities both at home and abroad.

YAMS – Young Adult Missionary Society consists of women ages 22 – 40 years old.

Job Descriptions

Organizational structure is designed to channel resources to meet the task and mission of the organization. As such, it must change as resources and tasks ebb and flow. Moses discovered that getting the people out of Egypt required one kind of leadership; leading them through the wilderness for 40 years required a completely different kind of leadership structure.

<u>Job Descriptions</u>

The First Church Organization

A church is a very special and unique creation. A "church" is considered a fellowship, which is one of the six core purposes of a church. Fellowship is gathering together as a church and uniting with other believers to encourage one another in faith. Church services, events, meals, small groups, classes and trips are all a part of fellowship. The other five purposes of a church include:

- Discipleship – Following Jesus, learning more about Jesus and the Bible
- Evangelism – Obeying God's command to love and serve unsaved neighbors
- Ministry – Serving others, sharing Christ's love, meeting needs, and teaching
- Prayer – Sincere conversations with God: alone, silent, aloud, in groups or in meetings
- Worship – Believers giving honor, glory and devotion to God

A church is an organism, which is a unit of life. There are people in many churches who will resist the idea of a church being organized. According to Charles Tidwell, some people think of organization as something out of place in a church. In the Old Testament, Book of Exodus, God uses Jethro, the father-in-law of Moses, to help Moses create the Bible's first chain of command. This biblical plan has been used by legal systems, armies and governments across the world to organize large groups of people and used to get things done in an efficient and effective manner.

Exodus 18:13-27, gives the account of Moses coming dangerously close to burning himself out. Moses was wearing himself thin Jethro, (Exodus 18:18, NIV). Moses' father-in-law came to his rescue. "You and these people who come to you will only wear yourselves out. The work is too heavy for you; you cannot handle it alone." Thanks to the common sense of Jethro, Moses was delivered from his own destruction of "burnout". There are three sections to Jetho's plan: mediate, communicate and delegate. First, Moses would *mediate* between the people and God (Exodus 18:19). Second, Moses would *communicate* God's message to the people (Exodus 18:20). Finally, Moses would *delegate* responsibility to others who would solve the day-to-day problems (Exodus 18:21). Moses would counsel the most serious problems. The teaching moment here is that through effective delegation a leader can multiply his or her effectiveness to meet the requirements of people in need.

Job Descriptions

Read these New Testament passages: Matthew 10:2-4, Mark 3:16-19, Luke 6:14-16, and Acts 1:13. These four passages outline the main order of the twelve disciples. In these lists one can observe that Simon Peter is always listed first, after Peter you will find James, John and Andrew not in any particular order. Now closely observe that Philip is always listed fifth, and then the order varies again with Bartholomew, Matthew and Thomas. Now in the third group of disciples, James, the son of Alphaeus, is always listed in the ninth position, and then the order varies again with Judas, the brother of James, Simon and Judas Iscariot. However, notice very carefully that Judas Iscariot is not named in the Acts 1:13. Is the picture getting clearer? There are three organized groups within the disciples. The first group of four disciples is headed by Simon Peter, the second group of four disciples is headed by Philip and the third group of four disciples is headed by James, the son of Alpheus. Review *table 3* below:

Group 1 Disciples	Group 2 Disciples	Group 3 Disciples
Simon Peter	**Philip**	**James, the son of Alphaeus**
James	Bartholomew	Judas, the brother of James (Thaddeus)
John	Thomas	Simon called Zelotes
Andrew	Matthew	*Judas Iscariot

Table 3: Biblical Organization of the Disciples

The organization of the disciples did not come from the nominating committee of the church, but by God Himself. The main objective to note in the Bible is that there seems to be some sort of organizational structure. Let's define and talk about the word "organization".

Definition of "Organization"

Organization is the arrangement of persons to get a job done. Webster defines organization as the act of being organized. Good organization includes what is to be expected and has a chain of command. In any organization there are three core elements: arrangement, people and a job.

Job Descriptions

Therefore, an organization is the arrangement of people to get a job completed. So what are the benefits of good organization?

Benefits of Good Organization

The benefits of good organization in any church can be found in Exodus 18:18. In this passage Jethro, the father-in-law of Moses, tells Moses that the tasks are too heavy for him (Moses) to perform alone. There are four core benefits of having good organization:

1. Good organization distributes the work.
2. Good organization places responsibility where it belongs.
3. Good organization reduces confusion.
4. Good organization helps avoid unnecessary duplication of effort.

Let's begin by discussing the first benefit of a good organization.

First, ***good organization distributes the work***. In the church, it is very difficult to try to accomplish all of the Lord's work alone. It takes a group of people to share the work. A healthy church organization is able to achieve its congregational goals in an effective manner. The church is not under-organized (struggling with how to get things done), nor is it over-organized (so organized that it gets inadequate congregational feedback). Carefully planned distribution leads to harmony, diversity, enabling and accountability.

   a) Harmony includes a balance maintained between organizational effectiveness (what to do) and efficiency (how to do it). Read Ephesians 4:3-4, which speaks about congregational unity and harmony.

   b) Diversity includes congregational distribution among diverse personalities, gifts, ministries and goals. (1 Corinthians 12:12). Great emphasis must be placed on communication and interaction as ways to encourage diversity.

   c) Enabling includes spiritual training to equip members for service. Members should use their spiritual gifts to help the lay leadership base grow. (1 Thessalonians 5:11).

   d) Accountability includes holding members responsible for their behavior and for their actions and duties to Christ and to one another. (Romans 14:12).

Job Descriptions

Second, ***good organization places responsibility where it belongs***. God has given each believer spiritual gifts that He will use for His glory. 1 Corinthians 12:7 says, "But to each one is given the manifestation of the Spirit for the common good. Man has educated himself with trained skills and abilities that can be used in the church to perform certain job functions. Such trained skills are accountancy, finance, security (patrol person), educator, etc. Philippians 1:6 says, "For I am confident of this very thing, that He who began a **good work** in you will perfect it until the day of Christ Jesus". Therefore, do not be afraid to let God use you. Be a good steward of your gifts. God says if you are faithful with few things He will make you a steward over many things (Matthew 25:23). 1 Peter 4:10 says, "As each one has received a special gift, employ it in serving one another as good stewards of the manifold grace of God." Use your gift or gifts at every opportunity to show the love, grace and power of God to others. This will produce fruit that remains and will glorify Him.

Third, ***good organization reduces confusion***. Moses did not have to carry the work load by himself after Jethro provided the organizational structure. Moses' work load became well distributed and evened out amongst his appointed leaders (Exodus 18:21). Moses was able to place responsibility where it belonged and confusion was minimized.

In Matthew 25:14-30, Jesus tells the parable of the talents. This is not specifically a parable on spiritual gifts, but one on stewardship and the grace of God in our lives. Spiritual gifts (also called "grace gifts") should be treated as such. A talent was a sum of money equal to about 15 years' wages. The master was leaving on a trip so he gave each of his three servants a different sum of money, according to their abilities, to invest while he was gone. To one he gave five talents, to another two, and to the last servant one talent. When he returned, only two of the servants had used the money, each of them doubling the amount given to him. The third servant was afraid and had buried his one talent. When the master came to him to settle accounts, the servant returned the only original amount of money. The master was furious that his servant did not use it at all. He had the "wicked, lazy" servant thrown out and gave his talent to the one with ten talents. This illustration shows us that Christ wants us to use the gifts He has provided us, not bury them. In verse 29 Jesus says, "For everyone who has will be given more, and he will have

Job Descriptions

an abundance." Whoever does not have, even what he has will be taken from him." In this passage, the illustration is of a job description: (talents) performance (servants' investments) and performance evaluation (settling of the accounts). The servant, who buried his talent, lost his talent; thus, confusion was minimized. When a group of people is given tasks, all are to work together equally for the common goal.

Finally, ***good organization helps avoid unnecessary duplication of effort***. Many times small churches do not have the resources to waste on doing things twice. This cannot always be said in larger churches. Sometimes, the left hand, does not know what the right hand is doing. There is a lack of communication.

The chart on page 27 illustrates the first biblical organization.

Names listed in the First Biblical Organization: Exodus 18:13-27

Jethro – Father-in-law to Moses

Aaron – Brother of Moses; became the first High Priest

Josephus – A Jewish historian and writer

Joshua – A close aid to Moses; one of the twelve sent by Moses to explore the land

Benjamin – A tribe of fighters

> Few elements of church management are as practical as organization. A healthy organization makes it easier for the church to excel. More can be accomplished with less energy expended. Ultimately, a church organization founded on Christ is the foundation of church success.

The First Biblical Organization: Exodus 18:13-27   Job Descriptions

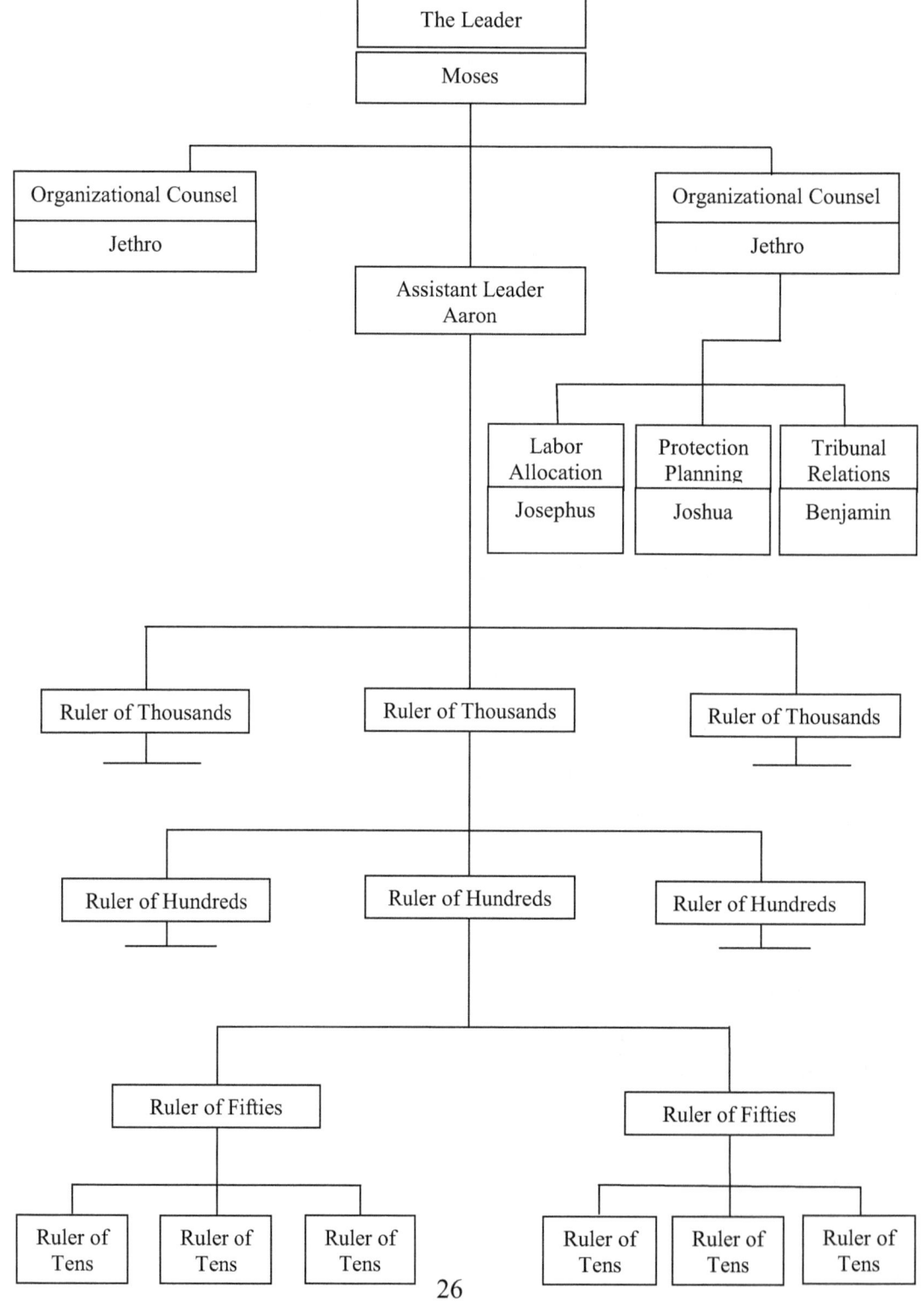

Job Descriptions

Called Versus Staff

Acts 9:5 – 9.
[5]And he said, "Who are You, Lord?" And He said, "I am Jesus whom you are persecuting, [6]but get up and enter the city, and it will be told you what you must do." The men who traveled with him stood speechless, hearing the voice but seeing no one. [8]Saul got up from the ground, and though his eyes were open, he could see nothing; and leading him by the hand, they brought him into Damascus. [9]And he was three days without sight, and neither ate nor drank.

The church expects certain positions to be evidence of a call to minister.

Such called positions are:

- Bishops
- Elders
- Apostles
- Pastors
- Ministers
- Deacons
- Ministers of Education
- Ministers of Music and,
- Many other ministering positions

These individuals should have a divine call. Any person with a divine call should also be presented to the church for a call by the church.

Staff

Staff positions are considered personnel committees such as office manager, secretary and other positions that allow spiritual gifts to be manifested in the church. Non-staff positions are considered auxiliary and committees within the church.

Ephesians 4:7-16

[7]But to each one of us grace has been given as Christ apportioned it. [8]This is why it says: When he ascended on high, he led captives in his train and gave gifts to men." [9](What does "he ascended" mean except that he also descended to the lower, earthly regions? [10]He who descended is the very one who ascended higher than all the heavens, in order to fill the whole universe.) [11]It was he who gave some to be apostles, some to be prophets, some to be evangelists, and some to be pastors and teachers, [12]to prepare God's people for works of service, so that the body of Christ may be built up [13]until we all reach unity in the faith and in the knowledge of the Son of God and become mature, attaining to the whole measure of the fullness of Christ. [14]Then we will no longer be infants, tossed back and forth by the waves, and blown here and there by every wind of teaching and by the cunning and craftiness of men in their deceitful scheming. [15]Instead, speaking the truth in love, we will in all things grow up into him who is the Head, that is, Christ. [16]From him the whole body, joined and held together by every supporting ligament, grows and builds itself up in love, as each part does its work.

Job Descriptions

"Structure is good in as much as it enables the church to meet the goals and objectives of her mission. However, when that is no longer the case, the church must call upon the living and powerful God who acts among and through his people to give new structures and a sense of resourcefulness equal to the challenges and worthy of the mission entrusted to the church."

-Ophelia Livingston

<u>Job Descriptions</u>

Organizational Structure for African Methodist Episcopal Zion Church

Job Descriptions

Organizational Chart
African Methodist Episcopal Zion Hierarchical Structure

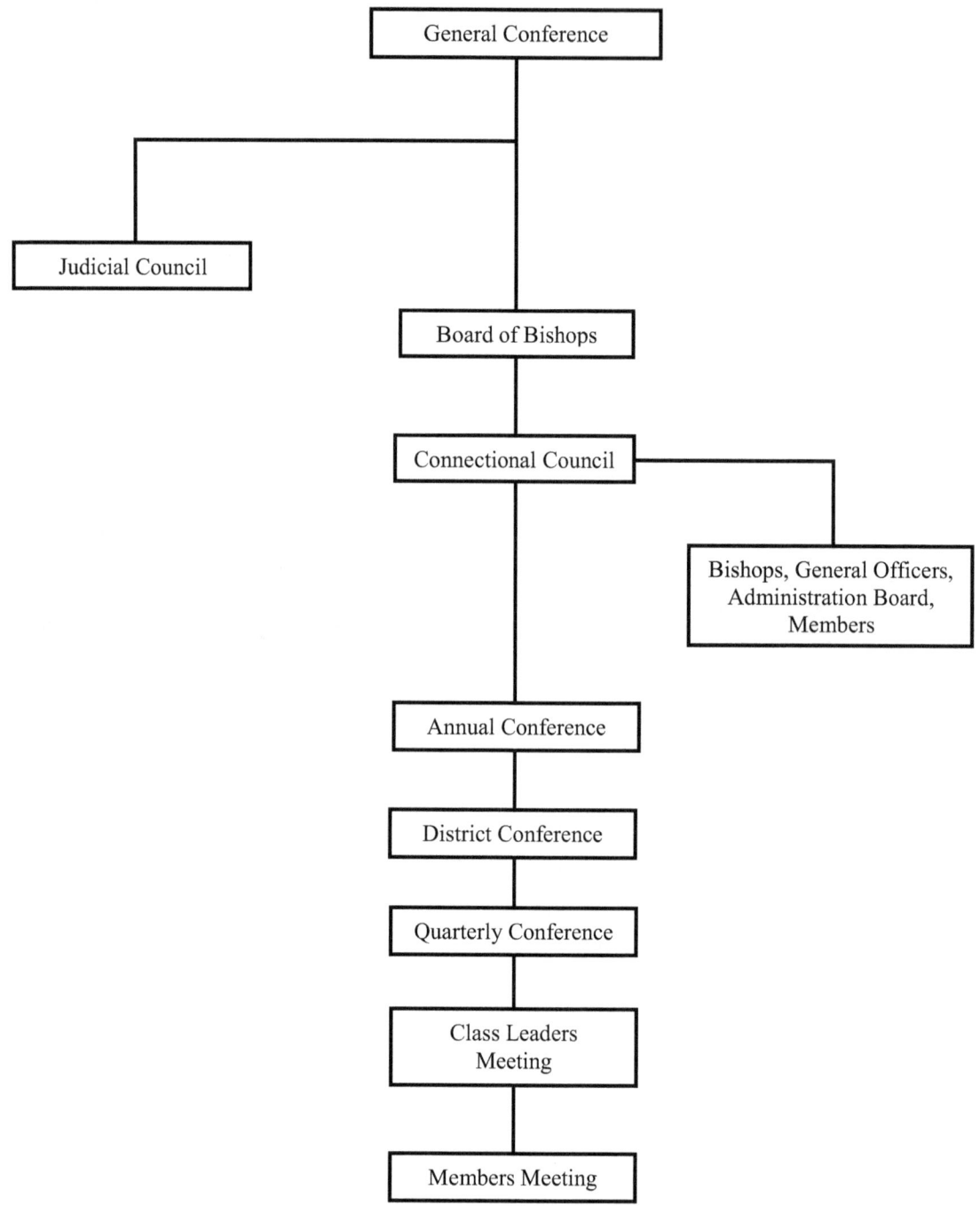

Job Descriptions
Christian Education Department (CED) Organizational Chart

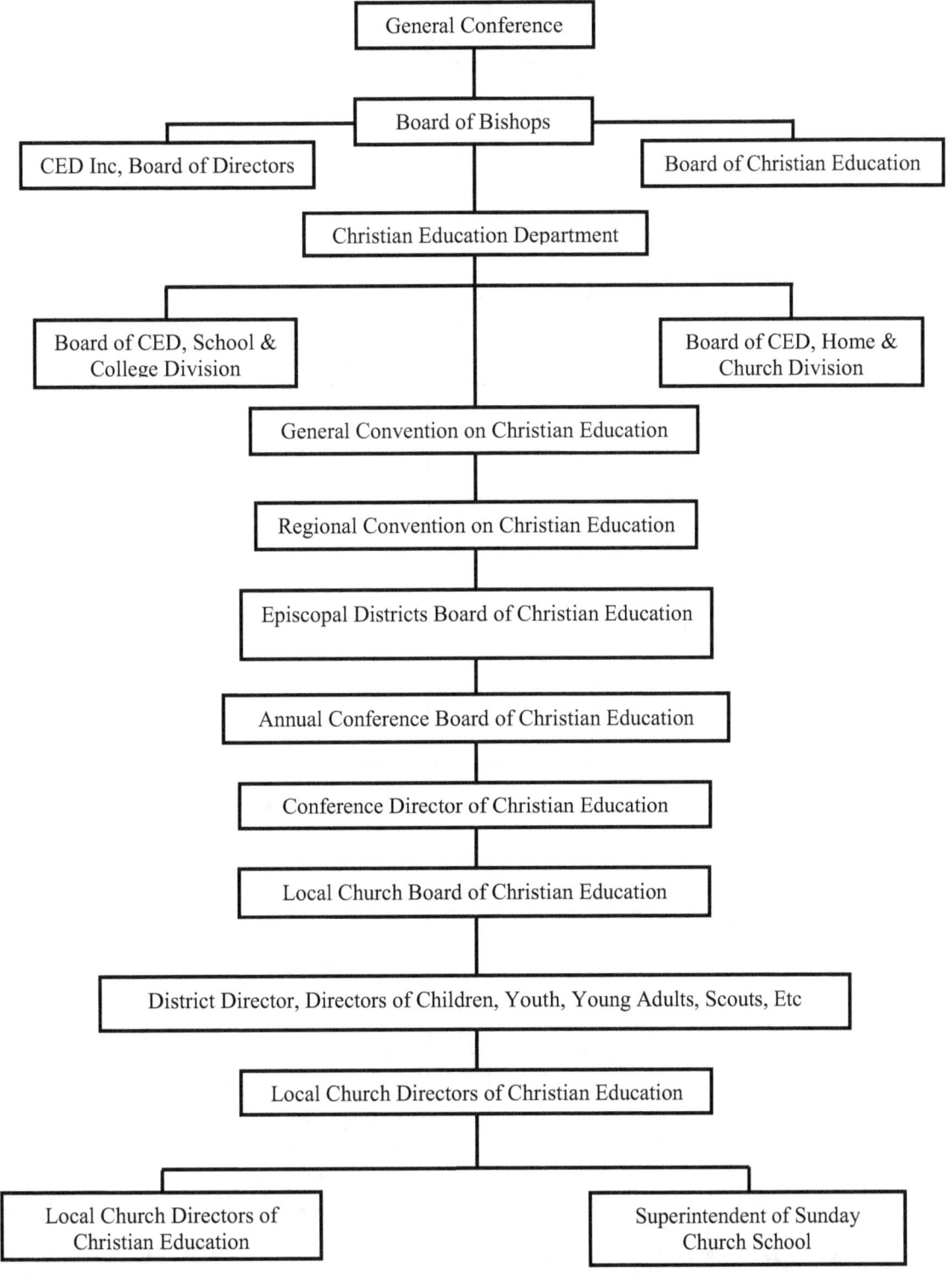

Job Descriptions
Women's Home and Overseas Missionary Society Organizational Chart

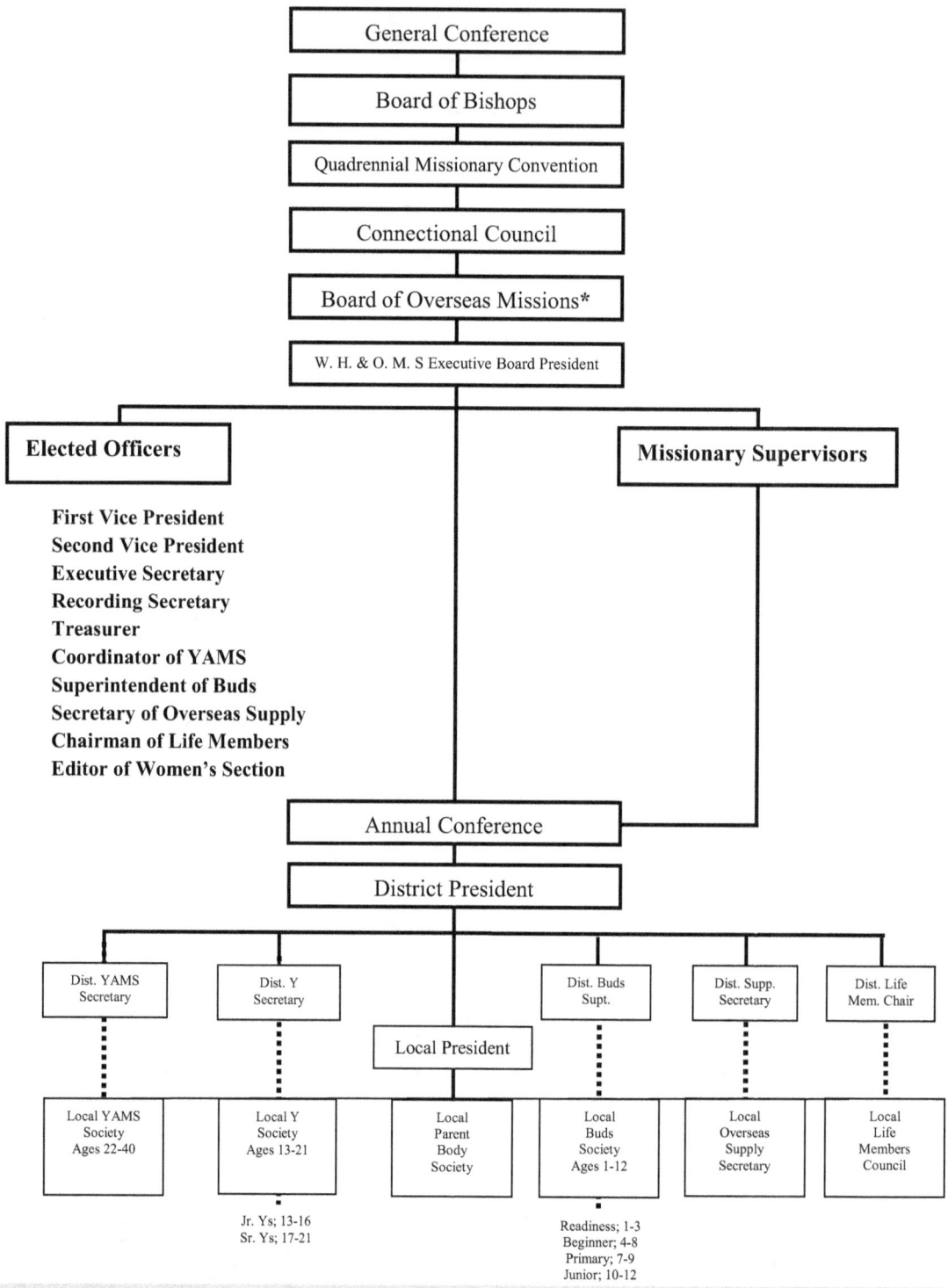

*The Chairman of the Board of Overseas Missions is the official contact of the W.H. & O.M. Society to the A.M.E. Zion Church

What Are Church Boards?

Responsibilities of the church board

Although the authority and responsibilities of church boards are as diverse as the churches they serve, there are some responsibilities that should be consistent and typical for all church boards. These are *establishing policy, financial reporting, compensation review,* and *budget approval.*

Why have church boards?

God designed His children to work together. The church is referred to as the body of Christ for good reason. We need each other. The good news is that well-managed boards, working together effectively and sharing their gifts, can help the pastor and accomplish the ministry of their churches in ways they never would have considered on their own.

The truth is, nothing will more quickly determine the success or failure of a leader in the local church than how well he/she works with the board. You can be an incredibly gifted preacher and sense a strong call of God on your life, but if you can't work effectively with your board, your ministry will never reach its full potential, and your church won't accomplish its mission.

<u>Job Descriptions</u>

And as we let our own light shine, we unconsciously give other people permission to do the same. As we are liberated from our fear, our presence automatically liberates others.

-Marianne Williamson

Job Descriptions

Boards

Trustee
Steward
Preacher's Steward
Poor Steward
General Claims' Steward
Junior Steward

Job Descriptions

Job Descriptions

Trustee

Title:
Trustee

Department/Ministry:
Board of Trustees

Job Summary:
The Trustee shall be at least 21 years of age, is nominated by the Pastor, and elected by a majority vote of the members of the local church. The number of Trustees shall be no fewer than three (3) and no greater than 15. The Trustees shall manage all of the temporal concerns not otherwise provided for and shall be responsible for all church property.

Report To:
Pastor-in-Charge

The Quarterly Conference is vested with the power to confirm the election of each trustee and to remove him or her from the office for just cause.

Principal Duties and Responsibilities:
1. *Uphold the mission of the church*
2. *Provide a place of worship*
3. *Protect the church property, physical equipment and all other assets owned by the church*
4. *Ensure that order and decorum are at all times observed*
5. *Ensure that all property is deeded to African Methodist Episcopal Zion Church*
6. *Perform duties of the Steward Board in its absence*
7. *Uphold the laws and practices of the church*

Other Duties and Responsibilities:
1. *Attend regularly scheduled monthly meetings*
2. *Attend regularly scheduled Sunday and weekday services*

Job Descriptions

3. Attend regularly scheduled Quarterly Conferences, Members' Meetings, and other church meetings as needed

Knowledge, Skills/Abilities, and Qualifications Required:

A: **Knowledge:**
1. Maintain knowledge of Methodist Doctrine and Discipline
2. Maintain knowledge of laws, polity, practices of the church as expressed in the "Book of Discipline of the A.M.E. Zion Church"
3. Maintain knowledgeable understanding of Property and Real Estate issues
4. Maintain care to the parsonage

B: **Skills/Abilities:**
1. Ability to witness to the gospel
2. Ability to lead and work in a multi-cultural environment
3. Ability to transact the temporal concerns of the church
4. Knowledge and understanding of property management to include: maintenance and repairs
5. Knowledge of Business Administration to include finances, investments, and recordkeeping

C: **Qualifications:**
1. At least twenty-one (21) years of age
2. Member in Full Connection
3. Member in good standing
4. Solid Piety

Acknowledgment of Review:

I have read the above, and understand that it is intended to describe the general content of and requirements for performing this job role. It is not an exhaustive statement of duties, responsibilities or requirements. I understand that the performance of other duties will be required from time to time in order to meet the needs of the church. I have been given a copy of this description.

Name:
_____Date:_____(mm/dd/yyyy)
    First Name   MI   Last Name

Job Descriptions

Steward

Title:

Steward

Department/Ministry:

Board of Stewards

Job Summary:

The Stewards, who shall number no less than three (3) or no more than nineteen (19), are nominated by the Pastor and submitted to the Quarterly Conference for confirmation. They shall serve for a term of one (1) year and may be nominated annually. They serve three tables – the table of the Lord, the table of the minister and the table of the poor.

Report To:

Pastor-in-Charge

The Quarterly Conference has the authority to confirm or reject the nominee.

Principal Duties and Responsibilities:

1. *Report accurate account of all expenditures or provisions collected for the support of the preachers in the circuit or station*
2. *Attend the Steward's regularly scheduled monthly meeting*
3. *Administer care to the Pastor and to the pastor's family*
4. *Administer care to the parsonage*
5. *Administer care to the needy*
6. *Attend regularly scheduled Quarterly Conferences and Members' Meetings of their circuit or station*
7. *Uphold the laws and practices of the church*

Other Duties and Responsibilities:

1. *Attend other church related meetings*

Job Descriptions

Knowledge, Skills/Abilities, and Qualifications Required:

- **A: Knowledge:**
    1. *Maintain knowledge of Methodist Doctrine and Discipline*
    2. *Maintain knowledge of laws, polity, practices of the church as expressed in the "Book of Discipline of the A.M.E. Zion Church"*
    3. *Apply needs of the Pastor and his/her family*
    4. *Maintain care to the parsonage*

- **B: Skills/Abilities:**
    1. *Ability to witness to the gospel*
    2. *Ability to lead and work in a multi-cultural environment*
    3. *Ability to transact the temporal concerns of the church*
    4. *Knowledge and understanding of property management to include: maintenance and repairs*
    5. *Knowledge of Business Administration to include finances, investments, and recordkeeping*

- **C: Qualifications:**
    1. *Member in Full Connection*
    2. *Member in good standing*
    3. *Solid Piety*

Acknowledgment of Review:

I have read the above, and understand that it is intended to describe the general content of and requirements for performing this job role. It is not an exhaustive statement of duties, responsibilities or requirements. I understand that the performance of other duties will be required from time to time in order to meet the needs of the church. I have been given a copy of this description.

Name:

_____Date:_____(mm/dd/yyyy)

    First Name   MI   Last Name

Job Descriptions

Preacher's Steward

Title:
Preacher's Steward

Department/Ministry:
Board of Stewards

Job Summary:
The Preacher's Steward is nominated by the Pastor. He/She is the Treasurer of the local church, responsible for all of the monies of the Board, and allocates the salary of the minister. Responsible for the support of the pastor in the local church.

Report To:
Pastor-in-Charge
The Quarterly Conference has the authority to confirm or reject the nominee.

Principal Duties and Responsibilities:
1. *Supervise the provision for the temporal support of the Pastor-in-Charge*
2. *Serve as Chairperson of the Board of Stewards*
3. *Provide the elements for the Lord's Supper*
4. *Provide the elements for the Lord's Feast*
5. *Meet the Class Leaders and Stewardess to be informed as to the comfort or necessities of the Pastor and his family.*

Other Duties and Responsibilities:
1. *Attend other church related meetings*
2. *Receive from the Leaders the money collected by them in their respective Classes*
3. *Report monies to the Leaders' Meeting*

Knowledge, Skills/Abilities, and Qualifications Required:

    A: **Knowledge:**
1. *Maintain knowledge of Methodist Doctrine and Discipline*
2. *Maintain knowledge of laws, polity, practices of the church as expressed in the "Book of Discipline of the A.M.E. Zion Church"*

Job Descriptions

       3. *Apply needs of the Pastor and his/her family*

       4. *Knowledgeable of Parliamentary Procedures*

B: **Skills/Abilities:**
1. *Ability to witness to the gospel*
2. *Ability to lead and work in a multi-cultural environment*
3. *Ability to transact the temporal concerns of the church*
4. *Demonstrate leadership ability, team building and organizational skills*

C: **Qualifications:**
1. *Member in Full Connection*
2. *Member in good standing*
3. *Solid Piety*
4. *Provide a genuine concern for the comfort of the Pastor and his/her family*

Acknowledgment of Review:

I have read the above, and understand that it is intended to describe the general content of and requirements for performing this job role. It is not an exhaustive statement of duties, responsibilities or requirements. I understand that the performance of other duties will be required from time to time in order to meet the needs of the church. I have been given a copy of this description.

Name:
_____Date:_____(mm/dd/yyyy)
    First Name   MI   Last Name

Job Descriptions

Poor Steward

Title:
Poor Steward

Department/Ministry:
Board of Stewards

Job Summary:
Is responsible for receiving and allocating (as the Pastor requests) monies collected for the needy.

Report To:
Pastor-in-Charge
The Quarterly Conference has the authority to confirm or reject the nominee.

Principal Duties and Responsibilities:
1. *Receive all monies collected for the benevolence (needy)*
2. *Provide the minister and stewards with names and addresses of the sick and needy members*
3. *Attend the Stewards' regularly scheduled monthly meetings*
4. *Attend and report at the Leaders' regularly scheduled monthly meetings*
5. *Attend and report at the Quarterly Conference*

Other Duties and Responsibilities:
1. *Attend other church related meetings*

Knowledge, Skills/Abilities, and Qualifications Required:
- **A:** **Knowledge:**
    1. *Maintain knowledge of Methodist Doctrine and Discipline*
    2. *Maintain knowledge of laws, polity, practices of the church as expressed in the "Book of Discipline of the A.M.E. Zion Church"*
    3. *Apply needs of the Pastor and his/her family*
    4. *Knowledgeable of Parliamentary Procedures*

Job Descriptions

B: **Skills/Abilities:**
1. *Ability to witness to the gospel*
2. *Ability to lead and work in a multi-cultural environment*
3. *Ability to transact the temporal concerns of the church*
4. *Demonstrate leadership ability, team building and organizational skills*

C: **Qualifications:**
1. *Member in Full Connection*
2. *Member in good standing*
3. *Solid Piety*
4. *Provide a genuine concern for the comfort of the Pastor and his/her family*

Acknowledgment of Review:

I have read the above, and understand that it is intended to describe the general content of and requirements for performing this job role. It is not an exhaustive statement of duties, responsibilities or requirements. I understand that the performance of other duties will be required from time to time in order to meet the needs of the church. I have been given a copy of this description.

Name:
_____Date:_____(mm/dd/yyyy)
    First Name   MI   Last Name

Job Descriptions

General Claims Steward

Title:
General Claims Steward

Department/Ministry:
Board of Stewards

Job Summary:
The General Claims Steward is responsible to receive all payments of General Claims and certify members in "Good Standing".

Report To:
Pastor-in-Charge

The Quarterly Conference has the authority to confirm or reject the nominee.

Principal Duties and Responsibilities:
1. *Receive all payments of General Claims*
2. *Report payments and amounts to the Church Treasurer, which is to be placed in the General Claims Treasury*
3. *Record and place on roll all persons who have paid General Claims as members in "Good Standing"*
4. *Issue cards certifying those who have paid General Claims as members in "Good Standing"*
5. *Responsible for all General Claims paid*

Other Duties and Responsibilities:
1. *Attend other church related meetings*
2. *Provide reports of General Claims' contributions upon request*

Knowledge, Skills/Abilities, and Qualifications Required:

A: <u>Knowledge:</u>
1. *Maintain knowledge of Methodist Doctrine and Discipline*
2. *Maintain knowledge of laws, polity and practices of the church as expressed in the "Book of Discipline of the A.M.E. Zion Church"*
3. *Maintain knowledge of banking procedures and practices*

<u>Job Descriptions</u>

    4.   *Maintain Membership Roll*

B: <u>**Skills/Abilities:**</u>

    1.   *Ability to witness to the gospel*

    2.   *Ability to work in a multi-cultural environment*

    3.   *Ability to transact the temporal concerns of the church*

    4.   *Demonstrate accurate record keeping*

C: <u>**Qualifications:**</u>

    1.   *Member in Full Connection*

    2.   *Member in good standing*

    3.   *Solid Piety*

    4.   *Honest*

    5.   *Act with complete integrity*

    6.   *Reliable*

Acknowledgment of Review:

I have read the above, and understand that it is intended to describe the general content of and requirements for performing this job role. It is not an exhaustive statement of duties, responsibilities or requirements. I understand that the performance of other duties will be required from time to time in order to meet the needs of the church. I have been given a copy of this description.

Name:

_____Date:_____(mm/dd/yyyy)

    First Name   MI   Last Name

<u>Job Descriptions</u>

Junior Steward

Title:
Junior Steward

Department/Ministry:
Board of Stewards

Job Summary:
Assist Stewards of the Church in their tasks and responsibilities

Report To:
Pastor-in-Charge
The Quarterly Conference has the authority to confirm or reject the nominee.

Principal Duties and Responsibilities:
1. *Assist/serve when called upon*
2. *Report his/her monthly collections to the Pastor*
3. *Provide provisions for the moving expense of the Pastor*
4. *Assist members in need*

Other Duties and Responsibilities
1. *Assist in the receiving of Sunday Morning offerings*
2. *Assist in the receiving of other worship service offerings*
3. *Attend training sessions*
4. *Attend Junior Steward meetings*

Knowledge, Skills/Abilities, and Qualifications Required:

    A: <u>**Knowledge:**</u>
        1. *Maintain knowledge of Methodist Doctrine and Discipline*
        2. *Maintain knowledge of laws, polity, practices of the church as expressed in the "Book of Discipline of the A.M.E. Zion Church"*

    B: <u>**Skills/Abilities:**</u>
        1. *Ability to witness to the gospel*

<u>Job Descriptions</u>

2. *Ability to lead and work in a multi-cultural environment*
3. *Ability to transact the temporal concerns of the church*
4. *Ability to receive directions*
5. *Ability to act in a respectful manner*

C: **<u>Qualifications:</u>**
1. *Member in Full Connection*
2. *Member in good standing*
3. *Solid Piety*

Acknowledgment of Review:

I have read the above, and understand that it is intended to describe the general content of and requirements for performing this job role. It is not an exhaustive statement of duties, responsibilities or requirements. I understand that the performance of other duties will be required from time to time in order to meet the needs of the church. I have been given a copy of this description.

Name:
_____Date:_____(mm/dd/yyyy)
    First Name   MI   Last Name

Job Descriptions

Class Leader

Title:
Class Leader

Department/Ministry:
Board of Stewards

Job Summary:
Class Leaders are defined as sub-pastors

Report To:
Pastor-in-Charge
Elected by the majority of the Quarterly Conference members present.

Principal Duties and Responsibilities:
1. *Attend Class Leader Meetings*
2. *Collect monies once every 90 days for the needy*
3. *Visit, counsel and make inquiry of members that are absent*
4. *Collect assessment for support of the presiding elder*
5. *Report visitation of absent members to the Pastor*
6. *Assist the Pastor-in-Charge*
7. *Devote care to the needy and distressed members*
8. *Administer to the needs of the members of the church*
9. *Report at the Quarterly Conference dues collected and duties performed*

Other Duties and Responsibilities:
1. *Attend regularly scheduled Leader's Meetings*
2. *Participate in on-call 365/24/7 emergencies*

Knowledge, Skills/Abilities, and Qualifications Required:
- A: **Knowledge:**
    1. *Maintain knowledge of Methodist Doctrine and Discipline*

Job Descriptions

    2. *Maintain knowledge of laws, polity, practices of the church as expressed in the "Book of Discipline of the A.M.E. Zion Church"*

    3. *Understanding of the Disciple Making Process*

B: **Skills/Abilities:**

1. *Ability to witness to the gospel*
2. *Ability to lead and work in a multi-cultural environment*
3. *Demonstrate leadership ability, team building and organizational skills*
4. *Provide sub-pastoral oversight and church governance*

C: **Qualifications:**

1. *Solid Piety*
2. *Mature experience*
3. *Ability to give religious counsel and advice wisely and affectionately*
4. *Ability to influence other members*
5. *Communicate spiritual concern and spiritual guidance to members*

Acknowledgment of Review:

I have read the above, and understand that it is intended to describe the general content of and requirements for performing this job role. It is not an exhaustive statement of duties, responsibilities or requirements. I understand that the performance of other duties will be required from time to time in order to meet the needs of the church. I have been given a copy of this description.

Name:

_____Date:_____(mm/dd/yyyy)

    First Name   MI   Last Name

Job Descriptions

Deaconess

Title:

Deaconess

Department/Ministry:

Board of Deaconesses

Job Summary:

The Deaconesses, who shall number no less than three (3) are appointed by the Pastor and confirmed by the Quarterly Conference. The Deaconess shall serve as long as long as there is no objection to her character or conduct.

Report To:

Pastor-in-Charge

Principal Duties and Responsibilities:
1. *Minister to the poor*
2. *Visit the sick*
3. *Pray with the dying*
4. *Care for the orphan*
5. *Seek the wandering*
6. *Comfort the sorrowing*
7. *Assist in preparation of the sacerdotal baptism and the elements of Altar dress*

Other Duties and Responsibilities:
1. *Attend regularly scheduled Deaconess Board meetings*
2. *Attend Quarterly Conference*
    a. *Monthly deaconess reports shall consist of the number of visits to homes, prisons and hospitals, number of church services and prayer services attended, number of candidates for baptism, number of Church Sunday School attendance, number of counseling appointments, number of prayers offered during home visits and number of pastoral assists during Communion.*
3. *Adhere to the Handbook for Deaconess of the A.M.E. Zion Church*

<u>Job Descriptions</u>

Knowledge, Skills/Abilities, and Qualifications Required:

    A: <u>Knowledge:</u>

        1. *Maintain knowledge of Methodist Doctrine and Discipline*

        2. *Knowledge of the Order of Service*

        3. *Knowledge of Sacerdotal Communion and Baptism*

    B: <u>Skills/Abilities:</u>

        1. *Ability to witness to the gospel*

        2. *Ability to pray*

        3. *Ability to transact the temporal concerns of the church*

        4. *Demonstrate team building and organizational skills*

    C: <u>Qualifications:</u>

        1. *Member in Full Connection*

        2. *Member in good standing*

        3. *Solid Piety*

        4. *Provide a genuine concern for the comfort of the sick and needy*

        5. *Communicate spiritual concern and spiritual welfare to members*

Acknowledgment of Review:

I have read the above, and understand that it is intended to describe the general content of and requirements for performing this job role. It is not an exhaustive statement of duties, responsibilities or requirements. I understand that the performance of other duties will be required from time to time in order to meet the needs of the church. I have been given a copy of this description.

Name:
_____Date:_____(mm/dd/yyyy)
      First Name   MI   Last Name

Job Descriptions

Stewardess

Title:
Stewardess

Department/Ministry:
Board of Stewardesses

Job Summary:
The Stewardess serves at the request of the Board of Stewards and assist the Class-Leader and Pastor-in-Charge in managing the spiritual duties of the church. Will have no legislative responsibility.

Report To:
Pastor-in-Charge

Principal Duties and Responsibilities:
1. *Provide support to Pastor and his/her family*
2. *Attend and prepare for female baptism*
3. *Work in conjunction with the Steward Board*
4. *Attend regularly scheduled Stewardess Board Meetings*
5. *Attend regularly scheduled Quarterly Conference*

Other Duties and Responsibilities:
1. *Provide needs to the parsonage*

Knowledge, Skills/Abilities, and Qualifications Required:

    A: <u>Knowledge:</u>
1. *Maintain knowledge of Methodist Doctrine and Discipline*
2. *Support the needs of the parsonage*
3. *Support the needs of the pastor and his/her family*

    B: <u>Skills/Abilities:</u>
1. *Ability to witness to the gospel*

Job Descriptions

    2. *Ability to assist with capital campaign development*

C: **Qualifications:**
1. *Member in Full Connection*
2. *Member in good standing*
3. *Solid Piety*
4. *Communicate spiritual concern and spiritual welfare to the Pastor and his/her family*

Acknowledgment of Review:

I have read the above, and understand that it is intended to describe the general content of and requirements for performing this job role. It is not an exhaustive statement of duties, responsibilities or requirements. I understand that the performance of other duties will be required from time to time in order to meet the needs of the church. I have been given a copy of this description.

Name:
_____Date:_____(mm/dd/yyyy)
    First Name   MI   Last Name

Job Descriptions

Lay Activities (Council)

Title:
Lay Activities (Council)

Department/Ministry:
Board of Lay Activities

Job Summary:
Provide the overall development and growth of the church and provide representation at all levels of the church.

Report To:
Pastor-in-Charge
The Quarterly Conference has the authority to confirm or reject the nominee.

Principal Duties and Responsibilities:
1. *Provide dissemination of information to the church members*
2. *Cultivate and embed loyalty in the church and provide spiritual life of the laity*
3. *Expand the denomination through education and evangelism*
4. *Promote the Kingdom of God in the church*

Other Duties and Responsibilities:
1. *Attend regularly scheduled Annual meeting*

Knowledge, Skills/Abilities, and Qualifications Required:

    A: **Knowledge:**
1. *Maintain knowledge of Methodist Doctrine and Discipline*
2. *Maintain knowledge of laws, polity, practices of the church as expressed in the "Book of Discipline of the A.M.E. Zion Church"*
3. *Maintain knowledge of Lay Activities (Council) Constitution and By-Laws*

    B: **Skills/Abilities:**
1. *Ability to witness to the gospel*

Job Descriptions

    2. *Ability to pray*

    3. *Ability to rally team and coach members*

    4. *Ability to organize church groups*

C: **Qualifications:**

    1. *Member in Full Connection*

    2. *Member in good standing*

    3. *Solid Piety*

    4. *Provide a genuine concern for the comfort of the sick and needy*

    5. *Communicate spiritual concern and spiritual welfare of others*

Acknowledgment of Review:

I have read the above, and understand that it is intended to describe the general content of and requirements for performing this job role. It is not an exhaustive statement of duties, responsibilities or requirements. I understand that the performance of other duties will be required from time to time in order to meet the needs of the church. I have been given a copy of this description.

Name:
_____Date:_____(mm/dd/yyyy)
    First Name   MI   Last Name

Job Descriptions

Local Director of Evangelism

Title:
Local Director of Evangelism

Department/Ministry:
Board of Evangelism or Evangelism Program of the Local Church

Job Summary:
Responsible for evangelism at the local church.

Report To:
Pastor-in-Charge

The Quarterly Conference has the authority to confirm or reject the nominee.

Principal Duties and Responsibilities:
1. *Direct the program of evangelism in the local church*
2. *Provide evangelism training for clergy and laity in the local church*
3. *Coordinate the evangelistic events of the local church*
4. *Implement strategic plans and policies of the local Board of Evangelism*
5. *Verify and validate that his/her name, physical address, email address, and phone number(s) are forwarded to the District Director of Evangelism*
6. *Prepare reports of his/her activities and submit them in a timely manner to the District Director of Evangelism*

Other Duties and Responsibilities:
1. *Attend Local Board and Evangelism meetings*
2. *Plan and coordinate evangelism events*
3. *Plan and coordinate outreach projects in the local church*
4. *Provide evangelism training in the local church*
5. *Attend District, Conference, Episcopal District, and Connectional Evangelism Events*
6. *Attend Quarterly Conference*
7. *Attend General Evangelistic Congress every four years*

Job Descriptions

Knowledge, Skills/Abilities, and Qualifications Required:

    A: **Knowledge:**

1. *An unyielding understanding of salvation by faith*
2. *A clear and accurate presentation of the gospel message*
3. *A clear understanding of Principal of Evangelism*
4. *A clear understanding of Disciple Making Process*

    B: **Skills/Abilities:**

1. *The gift of evangelism*
2. *The ability to lead*
3. *The ability to teach and train in evangelism and discipleship*
4. *A proven disciple maker*
5. *A passion for the souls of the lost*

    C: **Qualifications:**

1. *Member in Full Connection*
2. *Member in good standing*
3. *Solid Piety*
4. *A passion to reach out to the lost*

Acknowledgment of Review:

I have read the above, and understand that it is intended to describe the general content of and requirements for performing this job role. It is not an exhaustive statement of duties, responsibilities or requirements. I understand that the performance of other duties will be required from time to time in order to meet the needs of the church. I have been given a copy of this description.

Name: _____ Date:_____(mm/dd/yyyy)

    First Name   MI   Last Name

Job Descriptions

Christian Education Board Member

Title:

Christian Education Board Member

Department/Ministry:

Christian Education

Job Summary:

Provide the overall development and growth of the church and provide representation at all levels of the church.

Report To:

Pastor-in-Charge who shall be chairman

The Quarterly Conference has the authority to confirm or reject

Principal Duties and Responsibilities:

1. *To make adequate provision for the organization, guidance, and supervision of Christian Education of Children, Youth, Young Adults and of Adults in the local church.*

2.
    a. *To elect, upon the nomination of the Pastor, the Director of Education in the Local Church.*

    b. *To elect, upon nomination of the Pastor, the Director of Church Education in the Local Church, and with the concurrence of the Pastor, supervisory Christian Education officers and leaders; and all other officers, teachers and leaders of Christian Education organizations, such as: Sunday Church School, Varick Christian Endeavor Societies, Junior Churches, Scouts, Vacation and Weekday Church Schools.*

    c. *To elect, upon nomination of the Director of Christian Education in the Local Church, with the concurrence of the Pastor: the Director of Christian Education of Children, Director of Christian Education of Youth, Director of Christian Education of Young Adults and Director of Christian Education of Adults.*

    d. *To elect, upon nomination of the Director of Christian Education in the Local Church, in consultation with the Directors of the age group divisions and with*

Job Descriptions

concurrence of the Pastor, all other officers and teachers of Christian Education in the Local Church.

3.
   a. *In Churches not having a Director of Christian Education, the Christian Education Board shall elect, upon the nomination of the Pastor: a Superintendent of the Sunday Church School, Presidents of the Varick Christian Endeavor Societies, Scout Masters, Directors of Vacation and Weekday Church Schools, and the chief administrative officer of every other Christian Education organization in the Local Church.*
   b. *To elect, upon the nomination of the General Superintendent of the Sunday Church School, with the concurrence of the Pastor: the Associate and Assistant Superintendents and the Superintendent of Children, Youth, Young Adults and Adults Divisions.*
   c. *To elect, upon the nomination of the General Superintendent, in consultation with the Superintendents of the Children, Youth, Young Adults and Adult Divisions and with the concurrence of the Pastor: teachers and officers for their respective divisions.*

4. *To provide for the organization and maintenance of Council of Children's Workers, Christian Children's Fellowship, Christian Youth Council, Christian Youth Fellowship, Christian Young Adult Fellowship, Christian Young Adult Council, Christian Adult Council and Christian Adult Fellowship.*

5. *In cooperation with the Trustees of the Church, to provide adequate housing and equipment for the Christian Education work as a whole and for various divisions, departments and classes.*

6. *To see that every division, department, and class of the Church School is adequately supplied with Curriculum material prepared or approved by Christian Education Department.*

7. *To provide for an adequate budget for the Christian Education work in the Local Church as a whole and for the several divisions, departments and classes, and for the raising of the budget and the careful expenditure of same.*

8. *To provide for leadership education of officers and teachers, and of prospective officers and teachers.*

9. *To see that accurate records are kept and reports from the administrative and supervisory officers of Christian Education and from the officers of all Church School organizations.*

10. *To call for and approve regular reports from the administrative and supervisory officers of Christian Education and from the officer of all Church School organizations.*

Job Descriptions

11. To see that proper missionary and temperance education, social education and action are given emphasis in the Christian Education program of the Church.
12. To make available information regarding the work of our Schools, Colleges and Seminars.
13. To see that the Anniversary Days are properly observed: Christmas, Easter, Children's Day, Church School Rally Day, Varick Day, Joseph C. Price's Birthday and Women's Day.
14. To hold regular meetings for the purpose of receiving and acting upon reports and recommendations, and for the consideration and determination of all matters relating to the Christian Education work in the Church.
15. To remove for cause any administrative or supervisory Christian Education Officer or officer of the Church School organizations, upon recommendation of the Director of Christian Education in the local Church, and with the concurrence of Pastor (or, upon recommendation of the administrative head of the respective Church School organization, with the concurrence of the Pastor in the Church in which there is no Director of Christian Education); and to fill vacancies occurring during the year in any of the elective positions.

Other Duties and Responsibilities:
1. Host a Christian Education Workers' Conference consisting of the Pastor, the Directors of Christian Education and all officers, teachers and leaders of Church School organizations.
2. Attend Christian Education Board Meeting once a month
3. Attend special call meetings

Knowledge, Skills/Abilities, and Qualifications Required:

    A: **Knowledge:**
1. Develop structure of the Church and the Christian Education Department
2. Understand basic purpose of Christian Education
3. Provide community and church needs
4. Provide and maintain Church School curriculum materials

    B: **Skills/Abilities:**
1. Identifiable planning skills
2. Identifiable organizational skills
3. Ability to evaluate and recommend

<u>Job Descriptions</u>

    C: **<u>Qualifications:</u>**
1. *Member in Full Connection*
2. *Member in good standing*
3. *Solid Piety*
4. *Provide a genuine concern for the comfort of the sick and needy*
5. *Communicate spiritual concern and spiritual welfare of others*

Acknowledgment of Review:

I have read the above, and understand that it is intended to describe the general content of and requirements for performing this job role. It is not an exhaustive statement of duties, responsibilities or requirements. I understand that the performance of other duties will be required from time to time in order to meet the needs of the church. I have been given a copy of this description.

Name:
_____Date:_____(mm/dd/yyyy)
    First Name   MI   Last Name

Job Descriptions

Directors of Christian Education

Title:

Directors of Christian Education (Children, Youth, Adults, Young Adults)

Department/Ministry:

Christian Education

Job Summary:

Provide for the overall development and growth of the church; provide representation at all levels of the church.

Report To:

Pastor-in-Charge

The Quarterly Conference has the authority to confirm or reject

Principal Duties and Responsibilities:

1. *Unify the Christian Education work of Children, Youth, Young Adults & Adults in the local Church*
2. *Supervise the Christian Education work of Children, Youth, Young Adults & Adults in the local Church*
3. *Promote the Christian Education work of Children, Youth, Young Adults & Adults in the local Church*
4. *Eliminate overlapping and unnecessary duplication*
5. *Create and govern policies involving a cross-section of the congregation*
6. *Serve on the Christian Education Board*

Other Duties and Responsibilities:

1. *Attend Quarterly Conference*
2. *Attend regularly scheduled Christian Education Board meetings*

Knowledge, Skills/Abilities, and Qualifications Required:

    A: **Knowledge:**

        1. *Understanding of church structure*

Job Descriptions

2. Understanding of Christian Education Procedures
3. Ability to administer Christian Education curriculum
4. Prepare appropriate level of curriculum material
5. Knowledge of Parliamentary procedures (Robert's Rules of Order)

B: **Skills/Abilities:**

1. Ability to communicate and organize effectively
2. Demonstrate leadership skills
3. Monitor and evaluate teachers
4. Demonstrate administrative skills

C: **Qualifications:**

1. Member in Full Connection
2. Member in good standing
3. Solid Piety
4. Provide a genuine concern for the educational needs of the church

Acknowledgment of Review:

I have read the above, and understand that it is intended to describe the general content of and requirements for performing this job role. It is not an exhaustive statement of duties, responsibilities or requirements. I understand that the performance of other duties will be required from time to time in order to meet the needs of the church. I have been given a copy of this description.

Name:
_____Date:_____(mm/dd/yyyy)
    First Name   MI   Last Name

Job Descriptions

Superintendent of the Sunday Church School

Title:
Superintendent of the Sunday Church School

Department/Ministry:
Christian Education

Job Summary:
Oversee the general and specific supervision responsibilities for the administration of the Sunday Church School. Provide spiritual leadership for the Sunday Church School.

Report To:
Pastor-in-Charge and Board of Christian Education
The Quarterly Conference has the authority to confirm or reject

Principal Duties and Responsibilities:
1. *Oversee Sunday Church School*
2. *Provide supervisory authority with staff and in meetings*
3. *Attend regularly scheduled Christian Education Board meetings*
4. *Attend regularly scheduled Administrative Board meetings*
5. *Attend regularly scheduled Teachers' Conference*
6. *Attend regularly scheduled Quarterly Conference*
7. *Attend regularly scheduled Christian Education at District levels*

Other Duties and Responsibilities:
1. *Preside over the Teachers' and Workers' Meetings*

Knowledge, Skills/Abilities, and Qualifications Required:
- A: **Knowledge:**
    1. *Formulate structure of Sunday Church School*
    2. *Develop functions for the Administrative Board*

Job Descriptions

B: **Skills/Abilities:**
1. *Ability to communicate and organize effectively*
2. *Demonstrate leadership skills*
3. *Monitor and evaluate teachers*
4. *Demonstrate administrative skills*

C: **Qualifications:**
1. *Member in Full Connection*
2. *Member in good standing*
3. *Solid Piety*
4. *Provide a genuine concern for the educational needs of the church*

Acknowledgment of Review:

I have read the above, and understand that it is intended to describe the general content of and requirements for performing this job role. It is not an exhaustive statement of duties, responsibilities or requirements. I understand that the performance of other duties will be required from time to time in order to meet the needs of the church. I have been given a copy of this description.

Name:
_____Date:_____(mm/dd/yyyy)
  First Name   MI   Last Name

Job Descriptions

Sunday Church School Teacher

Title:
Sunday Church School Teacher

Department/Ministry:
Christian Education Board

Job Summary:
Provide teaching and training of prospective class level for spiritual growth

Report To:
Pastor-in-Charge and Board of Christian Education
The Quarterly Conference has the authority to confirm or reject

Principal Duties and Responsibilities:
1. *Teach his/her class level using prescribed teaching tools provided from Christian Education Board*
2. *Involve and challenge students in his/her class level through the study of Church School*
3. *Attend Teacher-Training Meetings and Workers Council*
4. *Maintain student attendance records*
5. *Notify Superintendent in advance in case of absence*

Other Duties and Responsibilities:
1. *Assist in Vacation Bible School studies*
2. *Attend regularly scheduled Teachers' and Workers' Meetings*

Knowledge, Skills/Abilities, and Qualifications Required:

    A: <u>**Knowledge:**</u>
1. *Knowledge and understanding of Sunday Church School*
2. *Knowledge of Sunday Church School material*
3. *Knowledge of lesson plans*

<u>Job Descriptions</u>

B: **<u>Skills/Abilities:</u>**
1. *Ability to communicate and organize effectively*
2. *Ability to motivate students*
3. *Ability to be creative in the classroom*
4. *Demonstrate Christian teaching skills*

C: **<u>Qualifications:</u>**
1. *Member in Full Connection*
2. *Member in good standing*
3. *Solid Piety*
4. *Provide a genuine concern for the educational needs of the church*
5. *Committed to Christian Education*

Acknowledgment of Review:

I have read the above, and understand that it is intended to describe the general content of and requirements for performing this job role. It is not an exhaustive statement of duties, responsibilities or requirements. I understand that the performance of other duties will be required from time to time in order to meet the needs of the church. I have been given a copy of this description.

Name:
_____Date:_____(mm/dd/yyyy)
    First Name   MI   Last Name

Job Descriptions

Missionary Society

To promote growth in the knowledge and understanding of God and His plan of redemption for the world as revealed through Jesus Christ and the power of the Holy Spirit.

Women's Home and Overseas Missionary Society
Local Coordinator of the Young Adult Missionary Department
Local Coordinator of the Young Adult Missionary Officers

Job Descriptions

<u>Job Descriptions</u>

Women's Home and Overseas Missionary Society

Local President

Title:

Women's Home and Overseas Missionary Society – Local President

Department/Ministry:

Departments of Women's Home and Overseas Missionary Society

Job Summary:

Supervise and promote the general interest of the Women's Home and Overseas Missionary Society.

Report To:

Pastor-in-Charge

The Quarterly Conference has the authority to confirm or reject

Principal Duties and Responsibilities:

1. *Preside at all meetings of the Society*
2. *Call extra meetings when necessary*
3. *Sign all drafts on the Treasury when ordered by the Society*
4. *Make reports as to the progress of the Department in the local church at the Mass Meeting*

Other Duties and Responsibilities:

Ensure that the program planned by the General Society, and given to her through the District President is implemented

Knowledge, Skills/Abilities, and Qualifications Required:

    A: <u>**Knowledge:**</u>

1. *Knowledge and understanding of the Women's Missionary Department*
2. *Knowledge of the total missionary mandate*

Job Descriptions

B: **Skills/Abilities:**
1. *Ability to communicate and organize effectively*
2. *Demonstrate leadership skills*
3. *Demonstrate administrative skills*

C: **Qualifications:**
1. *Member in Full Connection*
2. *Member in good standing*
3. *Solid Piety*
4. *Committed to missionary work*

Acknowledgment of Review:

I have read the above, and understand that it is intended to describe the general content of and requirements for performing this job role. It is not an exhaustive statement of duties, responsibilities or requirements. I understand that the performance of other duties will be required from time to time in order to meet the needs of the church. I have been given a copy of this description.

Name:
_____Date:_____(mm/dd/yyyy)

Job Descriptions
Local Coordinator of the Young Adult Missionary Department

Title:
Local Coordinator of the Young Adult Missionary Department

Department/Ministry:
Missionary Department

Job Summary:
Provide oversight of Young Adult Missionary Society to educate, train and unite women, ages 22-40 for mission service in the church and community. Coordinate mission services in the areas of child abuse, teen age pregnancies, drug dependency, world hunger, Christian growth, Christian witness and perpetuate the experience of W.H.&O.M.S.

Report To:
Pastor-in-Charge and Board of Christian Education
The Quarterly Conference has the authority to confirm or reject

Principal Duties and Responsibilities:
1. *Preside at all meetings of the Local Young Adult Missionary Society*
2. *Call extra meetings when necessary*
3. *Implement the program planned by the General Society, given to her through the District Coordinator for the Young Adult Missionary Society*
4. *Suggest programmatic ideas suited to the interest and age of the Young Adult Missionary Society*
5. *Report progress of the Department in the local church at the Mass Meetings*
6. *Prepare list of names and addresses of local Young Adult Missionary Society members and submit it to District President*
7. *Appoint various committees as suggested by the Constitution*

Other Duties and Responsibilities:
1. *Assist in Vacation Bible School studies*
2. *Attend regularly schedule Teachers' and Workers' Meetings*

<u>Job Descriptions</u>

Knowledge, Skills/Abilities, and Qualifications Required:

    A: **Knowledge:**

        1. *Knowledge of Young Adult Missionary Department Society and its material*

    B: **Skills/Abilities:**

        1. *Ability to communicate and organize effectively*

        2. *Demonstrate leadership skills*

        3. *Demonstrate administrative skills*

    C: **Qualifications:**

        1. *Member in Full Connection*

        2. *Member in good standing*

        3. *Solid Piety*

        4. *Provide a genuine concern for the Young Adult Missionary Department*

Acknowledgment of Review:

I have read the above, and understand that it is intended to describe the general content of and requirements for performing this job role. It is not an exhaustive statement of duties, responsibilities or requirements. I understand that the performance of other duties will be required from time to time in order to meet the needs of the church. I have been given a copy of this description.

Name:
_____Date:_____(mm/dd/yyyy)
    First Name   MI   Last Name

Job Descriptions

Local Coordinator of the Young Adult Missionary Officers

Title:

Local Coordinator of the Young Adult Missionary Officers

Department/Ministry:

Missionary Department

Job Summary:

Ensure that the program planned by the General Society and given to her though the District Coordinator for the Young Adult Missionary Society is implemented in the Local Church.

Report To:

Pastor-in-Charge,
Elected by the membership of the Society in each church

Principal Duties and Responsibilities:

1. *Preside at all meetings of the Local Young Adult Missionary Society*
2. *Call extra meetings when necessary*
3. *Suggest programmatic ideas suited to the interest and age of the Young Adult Missionary Society*
4. *Report progress of the Department in the local church at the Mass Meetings*
5. *Prepare list of names and addresses of local Young Adult Missionary Society members and report it to District President*
6. *Appoint various committees as suggested by the Constitution*
7. *Ready to answer, act, agree, or yield to the Quarterly Conference*

Other Duties and Responsibilities:

1. *Plan and prepare for meetings*
2. *Plan and prepare special programs*

Job Descriptions

Knowledge, Skills/Abilities, and Qualifications Required:

- **A:** **Knowledge:**

    Knowledge of Young Adult Missionary Department Society and its material

- **B:** **Skills/Abilities:**
    1. *Ability to communicate and organize*
    2. *Demonstrate e*
    3. *Effective leadership skills*
    4. *Demonstrate administrative skills*

- **C:** **Qualifications:**
    1. *Member in Full Connection*
    2. *Member in good standing*
    5. *Solid Piety*
    6. *Provide a genuine concern for the Young Adult Missionary Department*

Acknowledgment of Review:

I have read the above, and understand that it is intended to describe the general content of and requirements for performing this job role. It is not an exhaustive statement of duties, responsibilities or requirements. I understand that the performance of other duties will be required from time to time in order to meet the needs of the church. I have been given a copy of this description.

Name:

_____Date:_____(mm/dd/yyyy)

    First Name   MI   Last Name

Job Descriptions

Local Church Staff Member

Administrative Assistant
Music Director or Minister of Music
Church Musician
Church Secretary
Church Treasurer
Church Sexton

Job Descriptions

Job Descriptions

Administrative Assistant - Local Church Staff Member

Title:

Administrative Assistant

Department/Ministry:

Church Staff

Job Summary:

Must first have and maintain a close personal relationship with Jesus Christ. Be an extension of the ministry of the Pastor-in-Charge, particularly in the area of administration.

Report To:

Pastor-in-Charge who has the authority to dismiss for neglecting duties

Principal Duties and Responsibilities:

1. *Participate in church meetings and training*
2. *Receive, screen, and direct incoming calls*
3. *Place outgoing calls for the pastor*
4. *Prepare church reports as requested*
5. *Update master church calendar with all church events*
6. *Coordinate all church calendar events with church secretary*
7. *Work with church secretary to prepare worship bulletins for liquid crystal device (LCD) projection viewing*
8. *Prepares scripture text and announcements for LCD projection viewing*
9. *Order and maintain church supplies as needed*
10. *Maintain maintenance agreements for all office equipment*
11. *Maintain schedule of appointments for pastor and pastoral staff*
12. *Maintain a list of hospitalized church members, special prayer requests, deaths, births, and other special events.*

Other Duties and Responsibilities:

1. *Attend church administration training*

Job Descriptions

Knowledge, Skills/Abilities, and Qualifications Required:

- **A:** **Knowledge:**
    1. Knowledge of how to prepare well-written minutes for documentation
    2. Knowledge of church management software
    3. Knowledge of parliamentary procedure
    4. Knowledge of a word processing program
    5. Knowledge of the three P's:
        a. Proficient – skilled in leadership and inspiration
        b. Pastoral – have a caring heart, tact and diplomacy
        c. Positive – have a cheerful attitude toward the missions of the church

- **B:** **Skills/Abilities:**
    1. Strong interpersonal skills with the ability to relate to various personality types and age groups.
    2. Ensure working relationship with Pastor-in-Charge
    3. Ensure trust, integrity and encouragement
    4. Demonstrate proficiency in typing
    5. Demonstrate organizational skills
    6. Demonstrate administrative skills
    7. Demonstrate leadership skills
    8. Demonstrate computer skills

- **C:** **Qualifications:**
    1. Member in Full Connection
    2. Member in good standing
    3. Solid Piety

Acknowledgment of Review:

I have read the above, and understand that it is intended to describe the general content of and requirements for performing this job role. It is not an exhaustive statement of duties, responsibilities or requirements. I understand that the performance of other duties will be required from time to time in order to meet the needs of the church. I have been given a copy of this description.

Name:

_____ Date:_____(mm/dd/yyyy)

       First Name   MI   Last Name

Job Descriptions

Music Director or Minister of Music - Local Church Staff

Title:

Music Director or Minister of Music

Department/Ministry:

Worship and Music

Job Summary:

Responsible to the Pastor-in-Charge for the total music ministry of the church.

Report To:

Pastor-in-Charge

The Quarterly Conference has the authority to confirm or reject

Principal Duties and Responsibilities:

1. *Direct the planning, organizing, conducting and evaluating of a comprehensive music program by preparing groups, soloists and choirs for internal and external ministry*
2. *Work with the ministerial staff on special music needs in the total church program*
3. *Supervise the work of the music ministry staff*
4. *Work with the nominating committee to enlist and train leaders for the music ministry*
5. *Work with the pastor in selecting music for regular and special worship services - including weddings, funerals and special projects*
6. *Coordinate the music program with the organizational calendar and emphases of the church*
7. *Recruit new members for the music ministry*
8. *Monitor the purchasing, maintenance and replacement of all music-related equipment, supplies and instruments*
9. *Keep informed on music methods, materials, promotion and administration*
10. *Organize and maintain a personal library of organ/piano literature*
11. *Prepare an annual music budget for approval and administer the budget*
12. *Direct congregational singing at all regularly scheduled worship services*
13. *Plan and arrange an "Order of Service" for worship services*
14. *Cooperate with associational and state leaders in promoting activities of mutual interest*
15. *Provide administrative duties involving the entire music ministry*

Job Descriptions

16. Assist in arranging for substitute musician when not able to be present or for vacation time

Other Duties and Responsibilities:
1. Oversee regularly scheduled music ministry staff meetings
2. Attend and/or teach church music workshops and classes
3. Purchase and listen to professional CD's, tapes, etc.,
4. Write articles for church publications
5. Communicate with choir presidents or members via bulletins or newsletters

Knowledge, Skills/Abilities, and Qualifications Required:

A: <u>Knowledge:</u>
1. Ability to play musical instruments
2. Ability to teach multiple styles of musical arrangements

B: <u>Skills/Abilities:</u>
1. Ability to communicate and organize effectively
2. Demonstrate leadership skills
3. Monitor and evaluate music staff members
4. Demonstrate administrative skills
5. Ability to attend music workshops and/or conferences

C: <u>Qualifications:</u>
1. Member in Full Connection
2. Member in good standing
3. Solid Piety
4. Provide a genuine concern for the music program needs of the church

Acknowledgment of Review:

I have read the above, and understand that it is intended to describe the general content of and requirements for performing this job role. It is not an exhaustive statement of duties, responsibilities or requirements. I understand that the performance of other duties will be required from time to time in order to meet the needs of the church. I have been given a copy of this description.

Name:
_____Date:_____(mm/dd/yyyy)
    First Name   MI   Last Name

Job Descriptions

Church Musician - Local Church Staff Member

Title:

Church Musician

Department/Ministry:

Church Staff

Job Summary:

Will play a musical instrument (piano, keyboard, organ, percussion, etc.) for church choir(s) during regularly scheduled rehearsals, when requested, and during regularly scheduled worship services.

Report To:

Minister of Music

Pastor-in-Charge who has the ability to dismiss musician for neglecting duties

Principal Duties and Responsibilities:

1. *Play musical instrument during regularly scheduled rehearsals and regularly scheduled worship services*
2. *Receive direction and guidance from Minister of Music*
3. *Play musical instrument(s) upon request*
4. *Play during weddings, funerals and for special seasonal programs as requested*
5. *Organize and maintain a personal library of organ/piano literature*

Other Duties and Responsibilities:

1. *Provide needed services related to weddings, memorials, funerals for which sexton is compensated separately*
2. *Perform other duties and responsibilities as directed and negotiated within the limits of the position*

Knowledge, Skills/Abilities, and Qualifications Required:

A: <u>**Knowledge:**</u>

1. *Ability to play different styles of music*

Job Descriptions

    2. *Ability to coordinate and arrange music*

B: **Skills/Abilities:**
1. *Ability to attend music workshops and/or conferences*
2. *Ability to read music and play hymnals, anthems, spirituals, etc.,*
3. *Ability to be dependable, supportive and organized*

C: **Qualifications:**
May vary

Acknowledgment of Review:

I have read the above, and understand that it is intended to describe the general content of and requirements for performing this job role. It is not an exhaustive statement of duties, responsibilities or requirements. I understand that the performance of other duties will be required from time to time in order to meet the needs of the church. I have been given a copy of this description.

Name:
_____Date:_____(mm/dd/yyyy)
    First Name   MI   Last Name

Job Descriptions

Church Secretary - Local Church Staff Member

Title:
Church Secretary

Department/Ministry:
Church Staff

Job Summary:
Is the recording officer for the Local Church. Provides or oversees secretarial services for the Pastors, Assistant Pastors, and the Church. Functions as the church liaison.

Report To:
Pastor-in-Charge

Principal Duties and Responsibilities:
1. *Record and maintain accurate minutes of the Local Church meetings*
2. *Maintain registry of baptisms, church membership lists, and other archival materials*
3. *Distribute church bulletins*
4. *Receive church mail*
5. *Maintain register of all baptisms, marriages and deaths within the congregation*
6. *Communicate correspondence to announcement secretary*
7. *Communicate correspondence to church staff, members and volunteers when needed*
8. *Mail cards and other church related mail as needed*
9. *Attend church secretary training or church administrator training*
10. *Maintain church management software program*

Other Duties and Responsibilities:
1. *Provide service and assistance to the church and others in a punctual, friendly and courteous manner.*

Knowledge, Skills/Abilities, and Qualifications Required:

    A: **Knowledge:**
        1. *Knowledge of how to prepare well-written minutes for documentation*

Job Descriptions

2. *Knowledge of church management software*
3. *Knowledge of parliamentary procedure*
4. *Knowledge of word processing program*
5. *Knowledge of office procedures*
6. *Knowledge of the three P's:*
   a. *Proficient – skilled in leadership and inspiration*
   b. *Pastoral – have a caring heart, tact and diplomacy*
   c. *Positive – have a cheerful attitude toward the missions of the church*

B: **Skills/Abilities:**
1. *Ensure working relationship with Pastor-in-Charge*
2. *Ensure trust, integrity and encouragement*
3. *Demonstrate proficiency in typing*
4. *Demonstrate organizational skills*
5. *Demonstrate administrative skills*
6. *Demonstrative leadership skills*
7. *Demonstrate computer skills*

C: **Qualifications:**
1. *Member in Full Connection*
2. *Member in good standing*
3. *Solid Piety*

Acknowledgment of Review:

I have read the above, and understand that it is intended to describe the general content of and requirements for performing this job role. It is not an exhaustive statement of duties, responsibilities or requirements. I understand that the performance of other duties will be required from time to time in order to meet the needs of the church. I have been given a copy of this description.

Name:
_____Date:_____(mm/dd/yyyy)
    First Name   MI   Last Name

Job Descriptions

Church Sexton - Local Church Staff Member

Title:
Church Sexton

Department/Ministry:
Church Staff

Job Summary:
Responsible for the care and upkeep of church buildings, furniture and grounds. Create a setting conducive to worship, study, discussion, pastoral care and worship. Responsible for arranging annual clean-up days.

Report To:
Pastor-in-Charge who has the ability to dismiss for neglecting duties

Principal Duties and Responsibilities:
1. *Engaged in the church's emergency policies and procedures*
2. *Opening and closing buildings except when other persons are authorized to do so*
3. *Adjusting thermostats and lighting*
4. *Ensure that safety devices such as fire extinguishers, smoke detectors and emergency lights are inspected as required*
5. *Prepare meeting rooms with chairs and tables*
6. *Maintain church lawn care and grounds beautification*
7. *Order and maintain supplies for cleaning, maintaining and repairing buildings/grounds*
8. *Arrange snow/ice/debris removal from parking areas, sidewalks, steps, etc.*

Other Duties and Responsibilities:
1. *Provide needed services related to weddings, memorials, funerals for which sexton is compensated separately*
2. *Perform other duties and responsibilities as directed and negotiated within the limits of the position*

Job Descriptions

Knowledge, Skills/Abilities, and Qualifications Required:

    A: **Knowledge:**

        1. *Knowledge of repairs*

        2. *When handling chemicals or operating machinery, shall have the ability to read and understand instructions*

    B: **Skills/Abilities:**

        1. *Experience in cleaning and caring for a building*

        2. *Communicate with church staff, volunteers, members and guests.*

        3. *Ability to stand, bend, reach and move intermittently during work*

        4. *Ability to make rational decisions when circumstances warrant it*

    C: **Qualifications:**

        1. *Passion for good stewardship of the facilities God has given to the church*

        2. *Punctual and dependable*

Acknowledgment of Review:

I have read the above, and understand that it is intended to describe the general content of and requirements for performing this job role. It is not an exhaustive statement of duties, responsibilities or requirements. I understand that the performance of other duties will be required from time to time in order to meet the needs of the church. I have been given a copy of this description.

Name: _____ Date:_____(mm/dd/yyyy)

       First Name   MI   Last Name

Job Descriptions

Church Treasurer - Local Church Staff Member

Title:
Church Treasurer

Department/Ministry:
Church Staff

Job Summary:
Responsible for receiving, counting and depositing donations

Report To:
Pastor-in-Charge who has the ability to dismiss for neglecting duties
The Quarterly Conference has the authority to confirm or reject

Principal Duties and Responsibilities:
1. *Oversee the congregation's financial records*
2. *Prepare accurate financial reports*
3. *Prepare and present accurate reports of income and expenditure to the Quarterly Conferences and Members' Meetings*
4. *Disburse monies according to approved budget when authorized*
5. *Attend budgeting sessions*
6. *Maintain, safeguard and manage congregational financial resources*
7. *Comply with governing bodies*
8. *Oversee internal financial controls*
9. *Attend financial treasurer training*

Other Duties and Responsibilities:
1. *Attend Quarterly Conferences*
2. *Attend Members' Meetings*

Knowledge, Skills/Abilities, and Qualifications Required:
  A: <u>Knowledge:</u>
   1. *Knowledge of financial record-keeping*

Job Descriptions

      2. *Knowledge of regulatory record-keeping*

      3. *Knowledge of federal and state payroll reporting*

B: **Skills/Abilities:**

      1. *Understanding of computer software systems*

      2. *Identifiable business skills*

C: **Qualifications:**

      1. *Member in Full Connection*

      2. *Member in good standing*

      3. *Solid Piety*

      4. *Confidentiality, Integrity, and Reliability*

Acknowledgment of Review:

I have read the above, and understand that it is intended to describe the general content of and requirements for performing this job role. It is not an exhaustive statement of duties, responsibilities or requirements. I understand that the performance of other duties will be required from time to time in order to meet the needs of the church. I have been given a copy of this description.

Name:
_____Date:_____(mm/dd/yyyy)
    First Name   MI   Last Name

Job Descriptions

Worship

Acolyte Chairperson
Acolyte
Choir
Greeters
Ushers

Job Descriptions

Job Descriptions

Acolyte Chairperson - Local Church Member

Title:

Acolyte Chairperson

Department/Ministry:

Church Committee

Committee Summary:

Provide schedule and train church members who will perform the ceremonial duties.

Essential Functions:

1. *Provide acolyte training*
2. *Examine the attire of all acolytes to ensure that all are well-groomed*
3. *Ensure cassocks-albs are not soiled or wrinkled*
4. *Ensure minister's instructions are communicated to the acolytes in advance of the service*
5. *Ensure that a schedule is posted and that church secretary has a copy for inclusion in weekly church programs*
6. *Ensure proper notification to each acolyte of schedule through electronic media, phone call and/or posted web schedule*
7. *Analyze conduct of equipment*
    a. *Check length of tapers on candle lighters*
    b. *Remove any noticeable stains*
    c. *Ensure availability of tapers*
    d. *Ensure proper storage of all equipment*
8. *Observe all acolytes and equipment before each service*
9. *Recognize and award acolytes annually*

Acknowledgment of Review:

I have read the above, and understand that it is intended to describe the general content of and requirements for performing this job role. It is not an exhaustive statement of duties, responsibilities or requirements. I understand that the performance of other duties will be required from time to time in order to meet the needs of the church. I have been given a copy of this description.

Name: _____ Date:_____(mm/dd/yyyy)

    First Name   MI   Last Name

<u>Job Descriptions</u>

Acolyte – Local Church Member

Title:

Acolyte Member

Department/Ministry:

Church Committee

Committee Summary:

Provide and perform the ceremonial duties during regularly scheduled worship services

Essential Functions:

1. *Maintain proper formal dress attire*
2. *Maintain readiness of duties (15 minutes before service)*
3. *Maintain reverence and dignity of duties*
4. *Ensure proper handling of candle lighter*
5. *Ensure candles are lit at the designated time*
6. *Maintain awareness and alertness of duties during worship*
7. *Store candle lighter in designated storage area*
8. *Remove, hang and care for candle lighters*
9. *Refer to Acolytes Handbook for guidelines and procedures*

Acknowledgment of Review:

I have read the above, and understand that it is intended to describe the general content of and requirements for performing this job role. It is not an exhaustive statement of duties, responsibilities or requirements. I understand that the performance of other duties will be required from time to time in order to meet the needs of the church. I have been given a copy of this description.

Name:

_____ Date:_____ (mm/dd/yyyy)

      First Name   MI   Last Name

Job Descriptions

Greeter - Local Church Member

Title:
Greeter

Department/Ministry:
Church Staff

Job Summary:
Responsible to assist the elderly and physically challenged worshippers as they enter the church and/or use special equipment and designated areas of the church.

Report To:
Pastor-in-Charge who has the ability to dismiss for neglecting duties

Principal Duties and Responsibilities:
1. *Assist worshippers with small children as they enter church.*
2. *Inform worshippers of children's ministry and escort small children to children's church or nursery*
3. *Observe congregation for special needs and inform ushers and church officials of those needs*

Other Duties and Responsibilities:
1. *Maintain a pleasant personality*
2. *Maintain neat appearance and proper attire*

Knowledge, Skills/Abilities, and Qualifications Required:

    A: **Knowledge:**
1. *Understand the order of service*
2. *Review bulletin for any changes in the order of service*

    B: **Skills/Abilities:**
1. *Ability to have a pleasant personality*
2. *Ability to communicate with worshippers*

__Job Descriptions__

    3. *Ability to stand for long durations of time*

  C: **Qualifications:**

    1. *Member in Full Connection/Probation*

    2. *Member in good standing*

    3. *Solid Piety*

Acknowledgment of Review:

I have read the above, and understand that it is intended to describe the general content of and requirements for performing this job role. It is not an exhaustive statement of duties, responsibilities or requirements. I understand that the performance of other duties will be required from time to time in order to meet the needs of the church. I have been given a copy of this description.

Name:
_____Date:_____(mm/dd/yyyy)

    First Name   MI   Last Name

Job Descriptions

Usher - Local Church Member

Title:
Usher

Department/Ministry:
Church Staff

Job Summary:
Assume the responsibility to welcome the people of God to the House of God, especially Newcomers.

Report To:
Pastor-in-Charge who has the ability to dismiss for neglecting duties

Principal Duties and Responsibilities:
1. *Communicate and prepare with the head usher for special instructions*
2. *Report for duty at the designated time listed in your handbook or procedures manual*
3. *Provide church bulletin to worshippers as they enter church*
4. *Introduce yourself to guests or to people you do not know*
5. *Observe congregation for worshippers who suddenly become ill*
6. *Walk the worshipper down the aisle and provide the bulletin as the worshipper enters the pew*
7. *Arrange hymnals and all incidentals in their designated place after service*
8. *Observe and pick up any items or valuables left in the pews after service and return to church office*
9. *Wear identifying badge during service and return to storage after service*
10. *Walk worshippers to pew seating at the appropriate time.*
    a. *Do not seat worshippers during*
        i. *Call to Worship*
        ii. *Invocation*
        iii. *Scripture or Responsive Reading*
        iv. *Prayers*
        v. *Anthems*
        vi. *Special Selected Selections*
    b. *Do seat worshippers during*
        i. *Congregational Singing*
        ii. *Interludes*

__Job Descriptions__

      iii. Special Seating Intervals

Other Duties and Responsibilities:
1. *Notify head usher as soon as you know that you will not be able to serve on your assigned day. Assist in getting a substitute and provide name to the head usher*
2. *Participate in the worship hour*
3. *Exhibit a pleasant and friendly personality*
4. *Observe the Pastor-in-Charge for non-planned changes or special instructions*

Knowledge, Skills/Abilities, and Qualifications Required:

    A: __Knowledge:__
1. *Understand the order of service*
2. *Review bulletin for any changes in the order of service*

    B: __Skills/Abilities:__
1. *Ability to have a pleasant personality*
2. *Ability to communicate with worshippers*
3. *Ability to stand for long durations of time*

    C: __Qualifications:__
1. *Member in Full Connection/Probation*
2. *Member in good standing*
3. *Solid Piety*

Acknowledgment of Review:

I have read the above, and understand that it is intended to describe the general content of and requirements for performing this job role. It is not an exhaustive statement of duties, responsibilities or requirements. I understand that the performance of other duties will be required from time to time in order to meet the needs of the church. I have been given a copy of this description.

Name:

_____Date:_____(mm/dd/yyyy)

     First Name   MI   Last Name

Job Descriptions

Church Committee

Budget/Finance Committee
Bulletin Board Committee
Calendar Committee
Culinary Art Committee
Education Committee
Estimating Salary Committee
Evangelism Committee
Floral Guild
Worship Committee

Job Descriptions

*If you want to avoid criticism in the church:
do nothing, say nothing, be nothing.*

Job Descriptions

Committees

What are Committees?

A group of people officially delegated by the Pastor-in-Charge to perform a function, such as mentoring, reporting, negotiating or acting on a matter. A committee is also considered a small group of people to whom a larger group has delegated the power to act or formulate recommendations.

When forming a church committee, clergy must consider the focus of the committee and who should be appointed to lead the committee. A thought to consider is: How will the committee help the church grow toward it mission and vision statement? To help assimilate these values there are four categories of questions: function, formational, relational, and operative. As leader of the congregation, clergy should meet with committee leaders in a group session to discuss the four categories.

#	Function	#	Formational	#	Relational	#	Operative
1	What is the purpose?	1	How have we experienced the grace of God in our lives this week?	1	How can we best serve the needs of our congregation?	1	How should we be organized?
2	Why are we here?	2	How have we been able to extend God's love to others this week?	2	How can we grow together in love?	2	How will we make decisions?
3	What programs should be provided?	3	How have we grown in faith this week?	3	How can we grow together in our faith	3	How will we recruit leaders?
4	What is God calling us to do?					4	How do we support our committee?
						5	How do we grow larger?

Table 4: Four Categories for Help in Deciding Who Should Lead Committees

Note: *The key is not to focus on each category separately, but to blend and balance all four. As leaders, your time in the church should not only focus on operational and functional questions, but on formational and relational questions as well. At the conclusion of your discussion, you should be able to identify which category has more weaknesses than another. Through your* *group discussions you will discover how you might the shift focus to achieve balance among the four categories.*

Unlike job descriptions and roles, committees provide a list of duties the small group will perform. A less formal template is used when describing a committee. However, there are three (3) main areas that should be covered.

	Function	Description
1	Title	Title of Job Position/Role
2	Committee Summary	Two or three sentences in length
3	Essential Duties	The first three functions should be the core duties and responsibilities

Table 5: Template for Committees

In some religious organizations committee members do *not* rotate off the committee while in other religious organizations, committee members *will* rotate off of the committee. The latter method allows for greater usage of a congregation to participate and familiarize themselves in church activities. Most church members are familiar with non-rotating committees; therefore, an extended explanation is provided in the literature below.

What are Rotating Committees?

Are there any real advantages to using a rotation system for church committees? Some would argue against this kind of system. Those who argue against the rotation system would say that you lose good committee members through this system. Some in smaller membership churches would say that they do not have enough members to implement a rotation system. Still others would argue that you might have a chairperson that is not qualified if the rotation system is fully implemented.

In order to answer this question for your church, consider the following advantages of using the rotation system for church committees.

    a. **More members can serve.** Every church has a rich resource in its membership. Using the rotation system forces a church to look for and enlist members who have never served on committees. Since you have to rotate a certain number of members off a committee each year, you will have to find more members who are willing to serve. In most cases, members are willing to serve when asked.

b. **Leadership is distributed among more members.** A church that does not use the rotation system will often use the same leaders over and over. This writer has heard many church members complain that the leadership of the church is centered on too few people. Using the rotation system will help to develop more leaders as well as have more people involved in the decision-making processes of the church.

c. **More members can serve as chairpersons.** Because a chairperson eventually rotates off a committee, more members have the opportunity to serve as chairpersons. Admittedly, some members do not want to serve as the leader of a committee; but more who are willing and capable will be able to serve when the rotation system is used.

d. **Keeps some members from becoming too powerful.** If the rotation system is not used, a person could serve as chairperson of a committee—for instance, the Budget or Finance Planning committee—for many years. In this case, the person could become powerful enough to control the purse strings of a church. Another example is a person who serves as chairperson of the Personnel Committee for many years. He/She might begin to exercise authority that was never intended.

e. **Provides for the removal of ineffective members**. Some people do not make effective committee members, but they will not resign for fear of looking bad or disappointing some other members. Knowing that they will eventually rotate off the committee provides a graceful way to exit this situation.

Job Descriptions

Do's and Don'ts Tips of Committee Meetings

Do:

    Be courteous to all members.

    Only deal with the agenda issues or the problem at hand.

    Develop a kind, trusting relationship with other members of the committee.

    Be fair to everyone, even those who disagree with you.

    Disagree with diplomacy.

    Learn to be completely honest and open.

    Be ethical and show integrity.

    Plan and distribute an agenda in advance.

    Begin and end on time.

    List on the agenda only the items that can be covered in the allotted time.

    Understand the role of each member of the committee as it relates to other members.

    Have well-written minutes and confirmed attendance records of all committee meetings.

    Understand the committee's task(s) and function(s).

    Evaluate the purpose and work of the committee.

Do not:

    Lose your temper in a committee meeting.

    Place blame on others in the group.

    Get involved in personalities.

    Force your will on other members.

    Let anyone press your panic button, causing overreaction.

    Add more topics than can be discussed in the allotted time.

Job Descriptions

Budget/Finance Committee

Title:

Budget/Finance Committee

Department/Ministry:

Church Committee

Committee Summary:

Members of the Budget/Finance Committee shall maintain and provide financial guidance for the church

Essential Functions:

1. *Formulate church budget for approval of the membership*
2. *Serve as a clearing house for obtaining vouchers*
3. *Maintain church records*
4. *Review and monitor church finances*
5. *Provide to the church membership quarterly reports of activity between proposed and actual budget*
6. *Provide adjustments to the budget when it is expedient*

<u>Job Descriptions</u>

Bulletin Board Committee

Title:

Bulletin Board Committee

Department/Ministry:

Church Committee

Committee Summary:

Create bulletin boards appropriate to church information and events

Essential Functions:

1. *Set up and maintain church bulletin boards as a creative, inspirational, and meaningful ministry*
2. *Post on a bulletin board, quotes, sayings, and information on the occasion of special days*
3. *Prepare and utilize a bulletin board as a kind of "For Your Information" center, posting community announcements, job openings, church announcements, etc.*
4. *Prepare and utilize a bulletin board as a kind of "Look What We've Done" center, displaying clippings, articles, and information about the achievements of the church, its members and ministries, of District, Conference, or Connectional ministries and personalities, and of the Body of Christ in general*
5. *Prepare and utilize a bulletin board to keep the church aware of liturgical themes and emphases of the Christian calendar year*

Job Descriptions

Culinary Arts Committee

Title:
Culinary Arts Committee

Department/Ministry:
Church Committee

Committee Summary:
Maintain adequate supplies in the kitchen for church functions, prepares menus and meals for various church-wide functions, coordinates volunteers for kitchen related events, establishes kitchen use policies and oversees the use of the kitchen by other church groups. Ensure consistency in delivery and compliance with prevailing health laws. Members should have a fundamental desire to serve food at any church function.

Essential Functions:
1. *Consult with church leaders to determine the food service requirements of the church*
2. *Recommend policies and procedures related to food service for kitchen operation, meal scheduling and facilities usage*
3. *Communicate approved food service policies and procedures to the church*
4. *Recommend the required personnel for the culinary arts committee*
5. *Coordinate the food service operation to the church*
6. *Utilize "food service portion" guidelines in making recommendations for purchases*
7. *Appoint a food service director*
8. *Work with the Stewardship (Budget/Finance Committee) to ensure that culinary supplies and food service have financial support in the annual budget*

Job Descriptions

Estimating Salary Committee

Title:

Estimating Salary Committee

Department/Ministry:

Church Committee

Committee Summary:

A committee of three or more members conferring with the Pastor, to establish the pastor's salary.

Essential Functions:

1. *Communicates, establishes and prepares Pastor's Travel and Expense (T &E) expenditures when Bishop summons his presence in behalf of General Church*
2. *Communicates, establishes and prepares Pastor's fringe benefit package*
3. *Convene and chair a Special Conference composed of Quarterly Conference Members to determine the amount of salary that shall be paid to the pastor.*

Job Descriptions

Evangelism Committee

Title:

Evangelism Committee

Department/Ministry:

Church Committee

Committee Summary:

Work with the local Director of Evangelism to make evangelism an ongoing, priority ministry of the congregation to win people to a profession or a renewal of faith in Jesus Christ. Develop and implement ministries of membership care, growth in discipleship, and spiritual formation including distribution of devotional resources.

Essential Functions:

1. *Demonstrate concern for persons who are not members in any local church, the church's own inactive members, and the care of all its members*
2. *Responsibility shall include, but not be limited to, working with all organizations of the church to identify and **reach out**:*
    a. *to persons who are neither members nor active in a church*
    b. *helping persons share the good news of Jesus Christ*
    c. *keeping a current prospect file*
    d. *providing for visitation programs*
    e. *setting growth goals*
    f. *inviting persons to Christian discipleship in the worship services*
    g. *planning specific evangelism events and missions*
    h. *incorporating new members*

Job Descriptions

Floral Guild

Title:
Floral Guild

Department/Ministry:
Church Committee

Committee Summary:
Create a wonderful worship space through the gift of floral arrangement

Essential Functions:
1. *Recommend policies and procedures for acquiring, arranging, and disposing of flowers and decorations for worship services and special events*
2. *Recommend policies related to providing flowers for sick and bereaved members and special occasions for the church*
3. *Work with the Stewardship (Budget/Finance Committee) to ensure that the Floral Guild has financial support in the annual budget*
4. *Acquire, place and dispose of flower arrangements and special decorations.*
5. *Serve as a resource team in planning, designing and renovating storage area for floral and decoration space*
6. *Create a yearly flower chart for special occasion services, such as Easter, New Year, Holy Week, Christmas, Mother's Day, Father's Day*
7. *Optional: Attend floral design classes*

Job Descriptions

Worship Committee

Title:

Worship Committee

Department/Ministry:

Church Committee

Committee Summary:

Members of the Worship Committee shall oversee and supervise all groups associated with the worship services to include and not limited to:

- *Choirs*
- *Ushers*
- *Greeters*
- *Acolytes*

Essential Functions:

1. *Maintain and provide hymnals, song books and all worship materials for the congregation*
2. *Evaluate and suggest improvements to the pastor for the worship service*
3. *Develop guidelines and policies for choir members, ushers, greeters, acolytes and others who assist during the worship services*
4. *Oversee special days for choirs, ushers, greeters, acolytes and others who assist during the worship services*

Liturgical Colors

White:	Symbolizing purity and light
	Used for Communion, Baptism, Christmastide, Weddings, Eastertide, seasons of Trinity
Red:	Signifying blood, Christian zeal, work and ministry of the church
	Used for Pentecost, Thanksgiving Day, Church Dedications and Anniversaries
Green:	Symbolic of hope and growth of the Christian life
	Used for Epiphany, Pre-Lenten Season and seasons of Trinity
Violet:	Signifying penitence, watching and fasting
	Used for Lenten Season, Four Sundays of Advent
Black:	Signifies mourning
	Used for Good Friday and funerals\

Job Descriptions

A Basic Guide To
Do's and Don'ts
of Church Interview Questions

Job Descriptions
A Basic Guide To Do's and Don'ts of Church Interview Questions

It is the responsibility of every employer whether you are a church, religious organization, non-profit ministry, etc., to assure that all questions asked of prospective job applicants are lawful. An untrained or inexperienced interviewer (church staff) may inadvertently stray into questioning that seems reasonable but, in fact, is inappropriate and unlawful.

This interview guide covers interview topics and questions that church leaders and staff members should become knowledgeable with before scheduling interviews to avoid improper or unlawful interview questions.

Basic Church Interview Question Guidelines

Before beginning the interview process, prepare your staff with the Do's and Don'ts of interview questions. The following questions should not be asked of the applicant.

Note *that churches and other religious organizations may give preference to individuals of their own religion.*

Job Descriptions
Do's and Don'ts Etiquettes of Church Interview Questions

#	These questions should not be asked during the interview process
1	Do not ask questions about the applicant's race or color
2	Do not ask questions about the applicant's religion
3	Do not ask questions about the applicant's gender
4	Do not ask questions about the applicant's sexual orientation
5	Do not ask questions about the applicant's national origin
6	Do not ask questions about the applicant's age
7	Do not ask questions about the applicant's body build
8	Do not ask questions about the applicant's legal and financial matters
9	Do not ask questions about the applicant's military records
10	Do not ask questions about the applicant's disabilities

Table 6: Questions Not To Ak During An Interview

Race/Ethnicity: No questions about race or ethnicity are appropriate.

Religion: As noted, churches and other religious organizations may give preference to individuals of their own religion; all others are prohibited from asking questions about religion.

Gender: Generally, no gender related questions are appropriate.
- It is inappropriate to ask female applicants different questions than male applicants.

Job Descriptions

- It is inappropriate to ask married female applicants different questions than single female applicants.
- Questions regarding pregnancy or potential pregnancy should not be asked. Questions on childcare arrangements are not appropriate. (See below for lawful questions about reliability and job availability)

Sexual Orientation: Many state and local laws prohibit discrimination on the basis of sexual orientation.

National Origin: You may not ask where an applicant was born or where his/her parents were born. You may ask if the applicant is eligible to work in the U.S.

Age: The *Age Discrimination in Employment Act* bars discrimination against persons age 40 or over. Age-based recruiting efforts, such as "recent graduate," are unlawful as are any questions during the interview process that deter employment due to age.

Height and/or Weight Restrictions: Unless there is a demonstrable business necessity for such restrictions, these questions may support gender or national origin discrimination

Arrest and Conviction Records: Questions about an applicant's arrest record are improper. Questions about convictions may be asked, if job related. *Equal Employment Opportunity Commission (EEOC)* guidelines say that employers must have a business necessity for the use of conviction records in hiring decisions. (See www.eeoc.gov for details.)

Financial Status: Do not ask if the applicant owns or rents a home or car, or if wages have been previously garnished, unless financial considerations for the job in question exist. If consumer credit reports are used, the employer must comply with the *Fair Credit Reporting Act (FCRA)* amended May 22, 2009 and the *Consumer Credit Reporting Reform Act (CCRRA)* of 1996.

Military Record: Do not ask what type of discharge the applicant received from military service. You may ask whether or not the applicant served in the military, the period of service, rank at time of discharge, and type of training and work experience received in the service.

Job Descriptions

Disability: Do not ask whether or not the interviewee has a disability. You may ask whether or not the interviewee can perform the duties listed in the job description with or without a reasonable accommodation.

Job Descriptions

Do's and Don'ts Etiquettes of Church Interview Questions

Interview Topics	Unacceptable Questions	Acceptable Questions
Reliability & Attendance	• Number of children/ages? • What are your baby-sitting arrangements? • Do you have pre-school age children at home? • Do you have a car?	What hours/days can you work? Are there specific times that you can/cannot work? What was your attendance record on your last job? Do you have responsibilities other than work that will interfere with specific job requirements, including reliable attendance?
Citizenship/National Origin	• What is your national origin? • Where are your parents from? • What is your maiden name?	Are you legally eligible for employment in the U.S.? Have you ever worked under a different name?
For Reference Checking	• What is your father's surname? What are the names of your relatives?	Have you ever worked under a different name?
Arrest and Conviction	• Have you ever been arrested?	Have you ever been convicted of a crime? If so when, where, and what was the disposition of the case?
Religion	• Any inquiry into religious affiliation, including religious holidays observed, EXCEPT that churches and other religious organizations may give preference to applicants of their own religion	None, except as noted
Gender	• Do you wish to be addressed as Mr., Dr., Ms., Mrs., Pastor or Rev?.	None
Addresses	• What was your previous address? How long did you reside there?	None, except as such information may be required for authorized consumer reports, as noted above.
	How long have you lived at your current address?	
	Do you own your own home?	

Table 7: Do's and Don'ts Etiquettes During a Church Interview

Job Descriptions

Note: This interview guide is provided for instructional purposes only. It is not intended to be, and does not represent, legal advice in any form. If you require advice, it is suggested that you contact a competent legal professional to discuss the specifics of your circumstances and obtain the advice you require.

Job Descriptions

Notes

Notes

Job Descriptions

Notes

Notes

<u>Job Descriptions</u>

Job Descriptions

Notes

Notes

Job Descriptions

Notes

Job Descriptions

Notes

<u>Job Descriptions</u>

Join OWL Risk Management Consulting's Monthly Newsletter

❑ **YES, I WOULD LIKE TO JOIN THE MONTHLY NEWSLETTER**

_____
LAST NAME   **FIRST**   **M.I.**

_____
STREET ADDRESS:

_____
CITY/STATE/ZIP:

_____
EMAIL/ADDRESS

SEND INFORMATION TO: <u>OWLIVINGSTON@OWLRISK.COM</u>

CALL TODAY: 1-866-579-7475

FOR CONFERENCES, WORSHOPS AND SEMINARS CONTACT US:

OPHEIA W. LIVINGSTON
150 N STEELE STREET
SUITE 102
SANFORD, NC 27330
WWW.OWLRISK.COM

Job Descriptions

Triple J Publishing
1-866-579-7475
www.owlrisk.com
www.owlrisk.blogspot.com

www.ingramcontent.com/pod-product-compliance
Lightning Source LLC
Chambersburg PA
CBHW081218230426
43666CB00015B/2782